BULLETS AND BARBED WIRE

AN EXPLORATION OF WWII IN THE PACIFIC THEATER – FROM GUADALCANAL TO CAPE GLOUCESTER

DANIEL WRINN

D1608145

CONTENTS

OPERATION WATCHTOWER

OPERATION GALVANIC

OPERATION BACKHANDER

GET YOUR FREE COPY OF WW2: SPIES, SNIPERS AND THE WORLD AT WAR

Never miss a new release by signing up for my free readers group. Learn of special offers and interesting details I find in my research. You'll also get WW2: Spies, Snipers and Tales of the World at War delivered to your inbox. (You can unsubscribe at any time.) Go to danielwrinn.com to sign up.

In the first six months of a war with the United States, I will run wild and win victory upon victory. But then, if the war continues after that, I make no such guarantees.

— ADMIRAL ISOROKU YAMAMOTO

PREFACE

The first months of World War II were a disaster for the
United States. The Japanese caught the Pacific Fleet flat-
footed in Pearl Harbor at anchor. Their attack dealt a massive
blow to American naval power.

The Imperial Japanese forces took full advantage of the initiative. They made a lightning assault to take the Philippines,
Thailand, Guam, Singapore, the Dutch East Indies, New
Britain, Rabaul, and Hong Kong. They moved deeper into
China and took Burma and New Guinea. It was an unstop-
pable victory after victory, and the Japanese Empire seemed
invincible.

OPERATION WATCHTOWER

THE 1942 INVASION AND BATTLE FOR GUADALCANAL

INTRODUCTION

In early summer 1942, intelligence reported that a Japanese airfield was being constructed in the Solomon Islands near Lunga Point on Guadalcanal. This triggered a demand for immediate offensive action in the South Pacific.

Admiral Ernest King was the Chief of Naval Operations in the Pacific. He was the leading advocate in Washington for starting an offensive. His views were shared by Admiral Chester Nimitz, the commander-in-chief of the Pacific Fleet. Adm. Nimitz had already proposed sending the 1st Marine Raider Battalion to destroy a Japanese seaplane base on Tulagi. An island twenty miles north of Guadalcanal, across the Sealark Channel.

The Battle of the Coral Sea had interrupted a Japanese amphibious assault on Port Moresby, at the time the Allied base of supply in eastern New Guinea. The completion of the Guadalcanal airfield would signal the beginning of the renewed enemy advance to the south. This increased the threat to the lifeline of American aid to Australia and New Zealand. On July 23,1942, the Joint Chiefs in Washington agreed to seize the line of communications in the South Pacific. The Japanese advance had to be stopped at any cost.

The Joint Chiefs created Operation Watchtower and the plan to invade and seize the islands of Guadalcanal and Tulagi.

The Solomon Islands are nestled in the backwaters of the South Pacific. Spanish fortune hunters discovered these islands in the sixteenth century. No European powers saw any value in these islands until Germany expanded its colonial empire two hundred years later. In 1884, Germany decreed a protectorate over the Bismarck Archipelago, in northern New Guinea, and the northern Solomons. Great Britain jumped into action and established a protectorate over the southern Solomon Islands and annexed the remainder of New Guinea. By 1905, the British crown passed administrative control over its territories in the region to Australia and the domain of Papua. Its capital was at Port Moresby.

After World War I, Germany's holdings in the region fell under the administrative control of the League of Nations. The seat of the colonial government was at Rabaul on New Britain. The Solomons are 10° below the equator. Hot, humid, and plagued by torrential rains.

By late January 1942, Japanese forces had seized Rabaul and fortified it. The site was an excellent harbor and had several airfield positions. The Japanese carrier and aircraft losses at the Battle of Midway had caused the Imperial Japanese Headquarters to cancel their plan of invading Midway, Fiji, New Caledonia, and Samoa. But the plans to construct a significant seaplane base at Tulagi went forward. The new location offered one of the best anchorages in the South Pacific. Strategically located over five hundred miles from the New Hebrides and just short of eight hundred miles from New Caledonia, and only one thousand miles from Fiji. It was the perfect location.

The Tulagi outpost on Guadalcanal was evidence of a sizable Japanese force in the region. Starting with the 17th Army, headquartered at Rabaul, and enemy 8th Fleet, the 11th Air Fleet and the 1st, 7th, 8th, and 14th Naval Base

Forces, were also on New Britain. In early August 1942, Japanese intelligence units picked up transmissions between Noumea and Melbourne. Enemy analysts decided that Adm. Ghormley had ordered an offensive force to assault the Solomon Islands or at New Guinea. The warnings were passed to the Imperial Japanese Headquarters in Truk but were ignored.

AUGUST 1, 1942

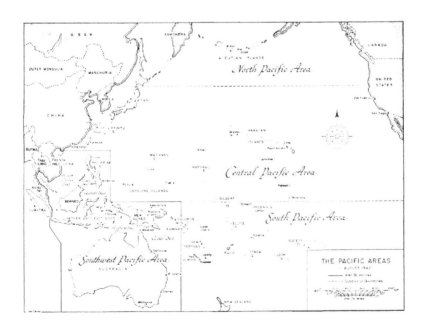

THE INVASION FORCE was on its way to targets in Guadalcanal, Tulagi, and the tiny islands of Tanambogo and Gavutu close to Tulagi's shore. The landing force would be composed of Marines. The covering and transport forces were supplied by the US Navy with the reinforcement of Australian warships. The 1st Marine Division was slated to make the landings. Five US Army divisions were located in the Southwest Pacific. Three in Australia, the 37th and 5th Infantry were in Fiji and an Americal Division on New Caledonia.

None of these divisions were trained for amphibious warfare, and all were vital parts of defensive garrisons in the Pacific. The 1st Marine Division began arriving in New Zealand in mid-June after the 5th Marines had reached Wellington. The rest of the unit's reinforced divisions were still preparing to embark. The 1st Raider Battalion was on New Caledonia, 1st Marines were at San Francisco, and the 3rd Defense Battalion was at Pearl Harbor. The 2nd Marine Division, who would eventually replace the 1st Division, 7th Marines, was stationed in British Samoa, while the rest loaded out from San Diego. The landing force infantry regiments all had battalions of artillery attached from the 11th Marines.

The news that this division would be the landing force for Operation Watchtower came as a shock to Maj. Gen. Alexander Vandegrift. He had expected that the 1st Division would have at least six months of training in the South Pacific before seeing any kind of action. Combat loading took precedence over any administrative loading of supplies. Equipment, weapons, ammunition, and rations were positioned to come off the ship with the assault troops. The combat troops replaced the civilian longshoremen. They unloaded and reloaded the cargo and passenger vessels often during rainstorms, which hampered the task, but the job got done.

All division forces got their share of labor on the docks as the various shipping groups arrived. Time was running out. Gen. Vandegrift convinced Adm. Ghormley and the Joint Chiefs that he would not meet the proposed D-Day of August 1, and only possibly meet the extended landing date of August 7.

An amphibious operation is a complicated affair when the

forces involved are assembled on brief notice from all over the Pacific. The pressure placed on Vandegrift was intense. The US Navy ships were the key to success, and they were scarce. The previous battles of the Coral Sea and Midway had damaged the Imperial Japanese fleet's offensive capabilities and crippled its carrier forces. But their enemy naval aircraft could fight as well ashore as afloat, and enemy warships were still numerous and lethal.

American losses at Pearl Harbor, Coral Sea, and Midway were considerable. The Navy knew their ships were in short supply. The day was coming when America's shipyards and factories would fill the seas with warships of all types, but they had not arrived in 1942. The name of the game for the US Navy was calculated risk. And now the risk seemed too great. The Operation Watchtower landing force might need to be a casualty. The US Navy never ceased to risk its ships in the waters of the Solomon Islands. This meant the naval lifeline to the troops ashore was stretched thin.

The tactical command of the invasion forces approaching Guadalcanal in early August was vested in Vice Admiral Frank Fletcher as the expeditionary force commander (Task Force 61). His forces consisted of the amphibious shipping carrying the 1st Marine Division, under Adm. Richmond Turner. Adm. Leigh Noyes contributed the land-based air forces that were commanded by Adm. John McCain. Fletcher's support forces comprised three fleet carriers, the *Wasp*, the *Saratoga*, the *Enterprise*, and the battleship *North Carolina*, six cruisers, sixteen destroyers, and three oilers. Adm. Turner's covering force included five cruisers and nine destroyers.

Onboard the transports approaching the Solomons, the Marines were expecting a tough fight. They knew little about any targets, even less about their opponents. The available maps were based on outdated hydrographic charts and information provided by former island residents. The maps based on aerial photographs were of poor quality and often mismapped.

On July 17, a couple division staff officers, Lieut. Col. Merrill Twining and Maj. William McKean, joined the crew of a B-17 flying from Port Moresby on a reconnaissance mission over Guadalcanal. They reported that they saw no extensive defenses along the beaches of Guadalcanal's north shore.

GUADALCANAL AND FLORIDA ISLANDS

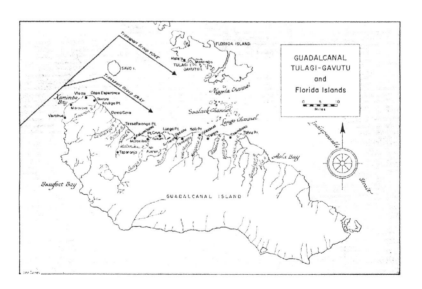

THE G-2 INTELLIGENCE OFFICER, Lieut. Col. Frank Goettge, determined that approximately 8,400 Japanese occupied Guadalcanal and Tulagi. Adm. Turner's staff concluded that the Japanese were around 7,000 men. In comparison, Adm. Ghormley's Intelligence officer put the enemy strength at just over 3,000 men. He was the closest to the actual total of

Japanese troops of 3,457 men. Over 2,500 of these men stationed on Guadalcanal were Korean laborers working on the airfield.

The Marine Corps had overwhelming superiority over the Japanese. The Marine Division had 19,514 officers and enlisted. This included the Naval Medical and Seabee engineer units. The infantry regiments numbered exactly 3,168 and had a headquarters company, weapons company, and three battalions. Each infantry battalion (933 Marines) was organized into a headquarters company, a weapons company, and three rifle companies. The artillery regiment had 2,581 officers and men. They were organized into 105mm howitzer and three 75mm howitzer battalions. A special weapons battalion of antiaircraft and antitank guns, a parachute battalion, and a light tank battalion contributed to additional combat power. An engineer regiment (2,450 Marines) with battalions of pioneers, engineers, and Seabees provided a hefty combat and service element. The total was completed by division headquarters, battalion headquarters, military police companies, and the division's service troops. The 1st Raider Battalion and the 3rd Defense Battalion had been added to Vandegrift's command to provide more infantry and a much-needed coastal defense for supplying antiaircraft guns and crews.

The 1st Division's heaviest ordinance had been left behind in New Zealand. Limited ship space and time meant that the division's big guns, 155mm howitzer Battalion, and all of the Motor Transport Battalion's 2 1/2 ton trucks were not loaded. Col. del Valle commanded the 11th Marines. He was distressed at the loss of his heavy howitzers. And equally concerned that the essential sound and flash ranging equipment necessary for effective counter-battery fire was left behind. There was not enough room for extra clothing, bedding rolls, and other supplies essential to support and reinforce the division for sixty days of combat. An additional ten days' supply of ammunition also remained in New Zealand.

In the opinion of several 1st Division historians and veterans from the landing, the men approaching the transports "thought they'd have a tough time getting ashore." They were confident young men and sure that they would not be defeated, but most men were entering combat for the first time. While there were combat veteran officers and NCOs within the division, most men were going to their first battle. The 1st Marines commanding officer Col. Clifton Cate estimated that over 90% of his men had enlisted directly after Pearl Harbor.

The fabled fame of the 1st Marine Division from the later World War II, Korean War, Vietnam War, and the Persian Gulf War—the most highly decorated division in the US Armed Forces—had not yet established its reputation. The convoy of ships, with its protective screen of carriers, reached Koro in the Fiji Islands on July 26. The practice landings did little more than exercise the transports landing craft since reefs prevented an actual beach landing.

The rendezvous at Koro gave the senior commanders a chance to have a face-to-face meeting. Turner, McCain, Fletcher, and Vandegrift got together with Ghormley, and Chief of Staff, Adm. Daniel Callahan. They learned that the 7th Marines on Samoa were to be prepared to embark on four days' notice to reinforce Operation Watchtower. Adm. Fletcher added some bad news to this. Because of the threat of land-based air assaults, he could not "keep the carriers in the area for more than forty-eight hours after the landing." Gen. Vandegrift protested he needed at least four days to get the division's gear ashore. Fletcher grudgingly kept his carriers at risk for another day.

On the 28th, the ships sailed from the Fiji Islands. They proceeded as if they were heading toward Australia. At noon on August 5, the convoy and its escorts turn north for the Solomon Islands. They were undetected by the Japanese. The assault force reached their target during the night of August 7 and split into two landing groups. The first was Transport Division X-Ray. They had fifteen transports headed for the north shore of Guadalcanal, east of Lunga Point. Transport Division Yoke followed with eight transports headed for Tulagi, Gavutu, Tanambogo in nearby Florida Island, which loomed over the other smaller islands.

Vandegrift's plans for the landing would put two of his infantry regiments—the 1st Marines and the 5th Marines—ashore on both sides of the Lunga River. They would be ready to seize the airfield and attack inland. The 11th Marines, the 3rd Defense Battalion, and most of the division's supporting units, would land near Lunga and be prepared to take advantage of the beachhead. Twenty miles across the Sealark Channel, the division's assistant commander, Brig. Gen. William Rupertus, would lead the assault forces to take Tulagi, Gavutu, and Tanambogo. The 1st Raider Battalion, 2nd Battalion, 5th Marines (2/5 Marines), and the 1st Parachute Battalion would patrol the nearby shores of Florida Island. The rest of Col. John Arthur's regiment would await orders in reserve.

They slipped through the channels on both sides of the rugged Savo Island. Heavy clouds and dense rain blinded the task force until the moon came out and silhouetted the islands. On his command ship, Gen. Vandegrift wrote to his wife:

Tomorrow morning at dawn, we land on our first major offensive of the war. Our plans have been made and God grant us our judgment has been sound. Whatever happens, I want you to know I did my best. Let us hope that will be good enough.

At 0641, on August 7, Turner signaled his ships to land the landing force. Just twenty-eight minutes before, *Quincy* started shelling the Guadalcanal beaches. When the sun came up that Friday at 0650, Marine assault troops touched down at 0909 on Red Beach, on Guadalcanal's north shore. To the men's surprise—and relief—no Japanese resisted the landing. The assault troops moved off the beach and into the surrounding jungle. They waded through the steep banked Ilu River and headed toward the enemy airfield. The 1st Marines that followed could cross the Ilu on a bridge the engineers had thrown up with an amphibian tractor bracing its middle. The silence was eerie. The absence of opposition worried the rifleman. The Japanese troops, mostly Korean laborers, fled to the west, terrified by a week's worth of B-17 bombardments, naval gunfire, and the imposing sight of the ships offshore. The situation was not the same across the Sealark. The Marines on Guadalcanal heard echoes of a firefight across the channel.

The Japanese on Tulagi would refuse to give up without a vicious, no surrender battle to the death. After the Marines landed, they moved inland toward the ridge that ran lengthwise through the island. The Marine battalions encountered pockets of resistance in the undergrowth of the island's thick vegetation. They maneuvered to outflank and overrun the opposition. The Marine advance was steady but ridden with casualties. By nightfall, they had reached the former British residency overlooking the Tulagi harbor and dug in for the night. They were across from the hill that overlooked the Japanese position—a ravine on the island's southern tip. The 2/5 Marines cleaned out its sector of enemy insurgents. By the end of their first day, the 2nd Battalion had fifty-six men killed and wounded. The 1st Raider Battalion's casualties was ninety-nine Marines.

During the night, the Japanese swarmed from hillside

caves in four separate ambushes, trying to penetrate the raider's lines. They were unsuccessful, and most died in their suicidal efforts. At dawn, the 2nd Marines landed and reinforced the attackers. By the afternoon of August 8, the mop-up was completed and the battle for Tulagi ended. The fight for tiny Tanambogo and Gavutu, both little more than small hills rising out of the sea connected by a one hundred yard causeway, had fighting just as intense as that on Tulagi.

The combat area was much smaller than the opportunities for fire support from offshore ships. Carrier planes were limited once the Marines landed on the beachhead. Naval gunfire began from the light cruiser *San Juan*. F4F Wildcats flying from the *Wasp* attacked enemy positions on the island. The 1st Parachute Battalion landed 395 men in three waves on Gavutu. The Japanese, with secured cave positions, opened fire on the second and third waves, pinning down the 1st Marines on the beach. Maj. Williams took a bullet in the lungs and was evacuated. Thirty-two Marines were killed under withering enemy fire. This time the 2nd Marines' reinforcements were really needed. The 1st Battalion's Company B landed on Gavutu and attempted to take Tanambogo. The attackers were driven to the ground and had to pull back to Gavutu.

After a rough night of fighting with the defenders of both islands, the 3rd Battalion, 2nd Marines, reinforced the men already ashore and mopped up each island. The Marines' butcher's bill on the three islands was almost 150. The wounded numbered just under 200. The surviving Japanese fled to Florida Island, which had been scouted out by the 2nd Marines on D-Day and found to be clear of enemy soldiers. The Marine landings and concentration of shipping in Guadalcanal waters acted as a magnet to the Japanese at Rabaul. Adm. Ghormley's headquarters was heard on D-Day, "desperately calling for the dispatch of surface forces to the scene" and to designate transports and carriers as targets for massive bombing. The messages were sent uncoded and emphasized the imminent danger of the threatened garrison. The Japanese response was quick and would be characteristic in the upcoming months of air and land battles to come.

On August 7, an Australian coastwatcher warned of a Japanese airstrike that was composed of light, heavy, and fighter-bombers fast approaching toward the island. Fletcher's pilots, whose carriers were positioned one hundred miles south of Guadalcanal, intercepted the approaching planes, twenty-five miles out, before they could attack Marine positions. This setback did not discourage the Japanese. Other aircraft and ships were en route to the inviting target.

On August 8, the Marines consolidated their positions ashore, taking the airfield on Guadalcanal and establishing a beachhead. Supplies were unloaded as fast as the landing craft could make the turnaround from ship to shore. Still, the men allocated on shore to handle the influx of rations, ammunition, tents, and aviation gas were woefully inadequate. The beach became a dumpsite. Just as the supplies were landed, they needed to be moved to other positions near Kukum Village and Lunga Point within the planned perimeter. Luckily, the lack of Japanese ground opposition allowed Vandegrift to shift the supply beaches west to a new beachhead.

Japanese bombers penetrated the American fighter screen on August 8. They dropped bombs from twenty thousand feet or higher to escape the antiaircraft fire. The enemy planes were inaccurate while they concentrated on the ships in the channel damaging several and sinking the destroyer *Jarvis*. In the fight to turn back the attacking planes, the carrier fighter squadrons lost twenty-one Wildcats.

The Japanese targeted the Allied ships. The Japanese commanders at Rabaul underestimated the strength of Gen. Vandegrift's forces. They thought the Marine landings were made up of a reconnaissance force of 2,000 men on Guadalcanal. By the evening of August 8, Vandegrift had 10,900 troops ashore on Guadalcanal and another 6,075 on Tulagi. Three infantry regiments landed with supporting 75mm howitzer battalions—the 2nd and 3rd Battalions. 11th Marines on Guadalcanal and the 3rd Battalion, 10th Marines on Tulagi. The 5th Battalion, 11th Marines' 105mm howitzers supported the assault.

Later that night, a cruiser force of the Imperial Japanese Navy reacted to the American invasion with an intense response. Adm. Turner had positioned three cruiser destroyer groups to block the Tulagi approaches. During the Battle of Savo Island, the Japanese showed their superiority of night assaults and fighting at this stage of the war. They smashed two of Turner's covering forces without any loss. Four heavy cruisers sunk—three American, one Australian—and another lost her bow. As the sun came up on what would soon be called "Ironbottom Sound," the Marines watched with grim faces as Higgins boats swarmed out to rescue survivors. American casualties were 1,300 sailors dead and another 700 wounded. Japanese casualties were less than 200 men.

The cruiser *Chokai* was the only Japanese ship to suffer damage in the encounter. The American cruisers *Vincennes*, *Astoria*, and *Quincy*, were sunk as well as the Australian HMAS *Canberra*. She was critically damaged and sunk by American torpedoes. Both the cruiser *Chicago* and the destroyer *Talbot* were damaged. Luckily for the Marines on shore, the Japanese force—five heavy cruisers, two light cruisers, and a destroyer—departed before dawn.

When the Japanese attack force leader, Vice-Admiral Gunichi Mikawa, returned to Rabaul, he had expected to receive the praise of his superiors. He got that, but he also found himself the subject of criticism. Adm. Yamamoto, the Japanese fleet commander, chided his subordinates for failing to attack the transports. Mikawa replied he didn't know Fletcher's aircraft carriers were that far off Guadalcanal.

This disaster prompted the American admirals to re-examine naval support for shore operations. Fletcher was concerned for the safety of his aircraft carriers. He'd already lost a quarter of his fighter aircraft. The expeditionary force commander had lost a carrier at Midway and Coral Sea. He felt he couldn't risk losing a third, even if it meant abandoning the men on the island. Before the Japanese cruiser attack, he got Adm. Ghormley's permission to withdraw.

The admiral told Gen. Vandegrift that Fletcher's impending withdrawal would have to pull out the amphibious force's ships. The Savo Island battle was essential in rein-forcing the decision to flee before Japanese enemy aircraft would strike. The next day the transports steamed away to Noumea. The unloading of ship supplies were interrupted while the ships fled. The forces ashore had seventeen days worth of rations—after counting Japanese food—and only four days' supply of ammunition for all weapons. The naval ships fled with most of the supplies and with the majority of the 2nd Division Marines still on board. The Marines were left at the island of Espiritu Santo in the New Hebrides. Col. Arthur and the Infantry Marines were distraught that they could not reinforce their comrades until they finally reached Guadalcanal on October 29.

Gen. Vandegrift ordered the remaining rations reduced to two a day for the Marines on the beachheads. Most of the Marines were smokers and now smoked Japanese brand cigarettes. The fast-burning tobacco scorched their lips because of the separate paper filters that came with the cigarettes.

The withdrawing naval ships also took with them precious, valuable engineering tools as well as some of the empty sand-bags. The Marines used discarded Japanese shovels to fill remaining sandbags. They strengthened their defensive positions along the beaches between the Tenaru River and the ridges west of Kukum.

A Japanese counter landing was a distinct threat. Inland of the beaches, Marines in foxholes had defensive gun positions, and they lined the west bank of the Tenaru. They maintained higher ground over the hills that faced west toward the Matanikau River and Point Cruz. South of the airfield were densely jungled ridges and ravines. The beachhead perimeter was guarded by outposts manned by combat support troops. Frontline positions included the engineers and amphibious tractor battalions. In fact, any Marine with a rifle—virtually every Marine—stood a night defensive duty. No place within the perimeter could be counted safe from enemy infiltration.

As Turner's transport sailed away, the Japanese began a pattern of harassing air attacks on the beachhead. Sometimes the raids came during the day. But the 3rd Battalion's 90mm antiaircraft guns forced the bombers to fly too high for effective bombing. The erratic pattern of bombs meant no safe place near the airfield, the preferred target, and no place could claim it was bomb free. Japanese air attacks became the new norm and severely harassed Allied positions, dropping bombs and flares indiscriminately.

The nightly visitors' aircraft engines soon became well-known sounds. They were called "Washing Machine Charlie" and later "Louis the Louse" when they signaled Japanese bombardment. When "Charlie" was used, it meant a twin-engine night bomber. "Louis" was a cruiser floatplane that signaled to the bombardment ships. But the harassed Marines use these names interchangeably.

Even though most of the division's heavy engineering equipment had disappeared with the naval transports, the resourceful Marines soon completed the airfield's runway with captured Japanese gear. On August 12, Adm. McCain's aide piloted in a PBY-5 Catalina. A flying boat landed on what was now officially Henderson Field, named for a Marine pilot,

Maj. Loftin Henderson lost at Midway. The Navy decided that fighters could use the airfield and flew off with several loads of wounded Marines. The first of 2,879 to be evacuated. Henderson Field was the centerpiece of Gen. Vandegrift's strategy. He would hold it at all costs.

The tiny airstrip was only two thousand feet long and lacked a taxiway and adequate drainage. Torrential downpours riddled the runway with potholes. It was rendered unusable but was essential for the success of the landing force. With the airstrip operational, supplies could be flown in and wounded flown out. At least in the Marines' minds, the lifeline of Navy ships was no longer available for the remaining Marines. Gen. Vandegrift's Marines were dug in on Henderson Field on the west and east.

The Imperial Japanese headquarters in Rabaul planned what they considered the most effective response to the Marine offensive. Their faulty intelligence estimated that the Americans had two thousand men. Several Japanese officers believed that a smaller force would quickly overwhelm the Marines' invasion. On August 12, CINCPAC determined that a sizable Japanese force was massing at Truk to steam to the Solomons and attempt to remove the Americans. The heavy carriers *Zuikaku* and *Shokaku* and the light carrier *Ryujo* were dispatched. After the stinging losses at Savo Island, the only significant American naval force increase in the Solomons was the new battleship, the *South Dakota*.

The Japanese Imperial headquarters in Tokyo had ordered Gen. Hyakutake's 17th Army to attack the Marine perimeter. For his assault force, he chose the 35th Infantry Brigade, commanded by Maj. Gen. Kawaguchi. Kawaguchi's primary force was in Palaus. General Hyakutake chose the 28th—a crack infantry regiment commanded by Col. Ichiki—to land first. Alerted for their mission while still on Guam, the Ichiki detachment assault echelon, one battalion of nine hundred men, was transported to the Solomon Islands on the only shipping available, six destroyers. The troops only carried small amounts of supplies and ordinance. A follow-on force of twelve hundred troops was to join the assault battalion on Guadalcanal.

BATTLE OF THE EASTERN SOLOMONS

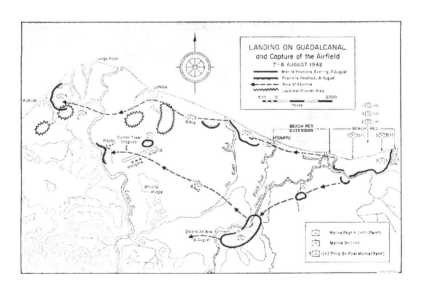

WHILE THE MARINE landing force headed to Guadalcanal, the Japanese were already on the island, providing an unpleasant reminder that they were full of fight. A Japanese captured naval officer told Marine officers that the Japanese group was ready to surrender near the village of Kokumbona, seven miles west of Matanikau. This was the area that Col. Goettge believed held most of the enemy troops who had fled the airfield. On August 12, a reconnaissance patrol of twenty-five men led by Goettge himself left the perimeter by landing craft. Their patrol landed near their objective. They were ambushed—and nearly wiped out.

Three Marines survived by swimming back to the lines. The rest of the other patrol Marines and their bodies were never found. After losing Goettge and his men, the perimeter became more vigilant. On August 14, a coastwatcher named Martin Clemens calmly exited the jungle and into the Marine perimeter. He'd observed the Japanese landing from the southern hills of the airfield and brought his bodyguard of native policeman with him. Jacob Vouza was a local and a retired sergeant major of the British Solomon Islands Constabulary. He volunteered his men to search out the Japanese east of the perimeter where they might have landed.

The news of Japanese sightings to the east and west of the perimeter were balanced out by news that more Marines had already landed. These Marines were aviators. On August 20, two squadrons of Marine aircraft groups were launched from the escort carrier *Long Island*, some two hundred miles southeast of Guadalcanal. Capt. John Smith led nineteen Grumman F4F Wildcats of the Marine Fighting Squadron onto the narrow runway in Henderson Airfield. Capt. Smith's fighters were followed by Maj. Richard Mangrum's Marine Scout-Bombing Squadron with twelve Douglas SBD Dauntless dive bombers.

They wasted no time. The Marine pilots were soon an action against the Japanese naval aircraft. Capt. Smith shot down his first enemy Zero fighter on August 21. Three days later, the Wildcats intercepted a strong Japanese aerial attack and shot down sixteen enemy planes. In this fight, Capt. Marion Carl, a Midway veteran, shot down three planes. The coastwatchers alerted the Cactus Air Force to an impending air attack. Thirteen of sixteen enemy bombers were engaged and destroyed. Three of the destroyed enemy dive bombers damaged three enemy destroyers attempting to reach Guadalcanal.

On August 22, five Bell P-400 Air Cobras of the Army's 67th Fighter Squadron landed at Henderson Airfield, followed later in the week by nine more Air Cobras. These Army planes had serious climb rate and altitude deficiencies. They would see the most action in ground combat support roles.

On August 24, the American attacking aircraft now included Navy scout bombers from the *Saratoga*'s Scouting Squadron. They turned back a Japanese reinforcement convoy of destroyers and warships.

This frenzied action became known as the Battle of the Eastern Solomons. Japanese destroyers had already delivered the vanguard of the Ichiki force at Taivu Point. A Marine patrol ambushed a substantial Japanese force at Taivu on August 19. The dead Japanese were quickly identified as Army troops. In the debris of their defeat, Marines found fresh uniforms and large amounts of communication equipment. This signaled a new phase of fighting. The Japanese encountered up to this point had all been naval troops.

Marines dug in along the Ilu River, often mislabeled as the Tenaru on Marine maps, and were ready for Col. Ichiki. The Japanese commander's orders were to "quickly recapture and maintain the airfield at Guadalcanal," in his own directive, his troops were to fight "to the last breath of the last man." And that is what they did.

Col. Ichiki decided to not wait for the rest of his regiment. Sure of the fact he only faced two thousand Marines, Ichiki marched out from Taivu to the Marine lines. Before he attacked, a bloody figure stumbled out of the jungle with a warning that the Japanese were coming.

Sergeant Major Vouza had been captured by the Japanese.

They found a small American flag hidden in his loincloth. The Japanese tortured him to get more information on the details of the Marine Invasion Force. He was tied to a tree, bayoneted twice through the chest, and beaten with rifle butts. Sergeant Major Vouza showed true grit as he chewed through his bindings to escape.

He was taken to Col. Edwin Pollock, whose 2nd Battalion, 1st Marines held the Ilu River mouth defenses. He warned that over five hundred Japanese soldiers were close behind him. The sergeant was rushed to an aid station and then the division hospital. He miraculously survived his ordeal and was awarded the Silver Star for his heroic actions. Sgt. Major Vouza was also made an honorary sergeant major of the US Marines.

On August 21 at 0130, Japanese troops stormed the Marines' lines in the screaming frenzy display of "spiritual strength," to destroy their weak American enemy. As the Japanese charged across the sandbar, astride the river Ilu's mouth. The US Marines cut them down. After a mortar assault, the Japanese tried again to storm past the sandbar. A section of 37mm guns pounded the enemy force with lethal effect. The 1st Battalion, 1st Marines, moved upstream at daybreak. And waded across the sluggish fifty-foot wide stream and moved to flank the Japanese. Wildcats strafed the beleaguered enemy force. Five light tanks blasted the retreating Japanese. By 1700—as the sun was setting—the battle ended.

Col. Ichiki, disgraced by defeat, burned his regimental colors and shot himself in the face. Eight hundred Japanese soldiers joined him in his ritual suicidal death. The few survivors fled eastward toward Taivu Point. Japanese Adm. Tanaka, whose reinforcement troops of destroyers and transports were responsible for the Japanese troop build-up on Guadalcanal, remarked about this foolish unsupported attack:

This tragedy should have taught us the hopelessness of bamboo spear tactics.

Col. Ichiki's overconfidence was a common trait, and weakness, among Japanese Army commanders. After the 1st Marines' fight with the Ichiki detachment, Gen. Vandegrift was inspired to write, and recalled:

These youngsters are the darndest people when they get started.

The Marines on Guadalcanal, both veteran and newly enlisted, were becoming fast accomplished jungle fighters. No longer were they "trigger-happy" as many had been in the first days ashore, shooting at shadows and imagined enemy. They were now waiting for targets, patrolling with enthusiasm, and more sure of themselves. The miscalled battle of the Tenaru had cost the regiment thirty-four killed in action and seventy-five wounded. Most of the division's Marines were now bloodied. What the men on Tenaru, Gavutu, Tulagi, and those of the Ilu had proved was that the 1st Marine Division could and would hold fast to what it had done.

While the 1st Division's Marines and sailors got a breather as the Japanese regrouped for another attack, the action in the air over the Solomon's intensified. Every day, Japanese aircraft arrived before noon to bomb the perimeter. Marine fighter pilots fought the twin-engine Betty bombers as easy targets. Japanese Zero fighters were another story. While the Wildcats were a much sturdier aircraft, the Japanese Zeros advanced speed and better maneuverability gave them an advantage in a dogfight. The American planes, when warned by the coast-watchers of Japanese attacks, had time to climb above the oncoming enemy and attacked by making firing runs during high-speed dives. These tactics made the airspace over the Solomon Islands dangerous for the Japanese. On August 29, the carrier *Ryujo* launched aircraft for a strike against the airstrip.

Capt. Smith's Wildcats shot down sixteen with a loss of four. Japanese air assaults continue to strike at Henderson Airfield without letting up. Two days after the *Ryujo* raid, Japanese bombers inflicted massive damage to the airfield. They set aviation fuel ablaze in incinerated parked aircraft. The Marine retaliation was to shoot down another thirteen enemy planes.

On August 30, two more MAG-23 squadrons flew into Henderson Airfield. These reinforcements were more than welcome. The frequent damage caused by combat attrition with scant facilities to repair and no access to parts kept the number of aircraft available a diminishing resource.

Gen. Vandegrift needed infantry reinforcements as much as he needed additional aircraft. He brought the now combined Parachute and Raider Battalions, under the command of the 2/5 Marines, over to Guadalcanal from Tulagi.

The division commander ordered a significant increase in reconnaissance patrols to search and destroy Japanese soldiers. On August 27, the 1st Battalion, 5th Marines made a landing near Kokumbona and marched back to the beachhead with no results. While the Japanese dug in out beyond the Matanikau, they waited and watched for a better opportunity to attack.

COL. EDSON'S BLOODY RIDGE

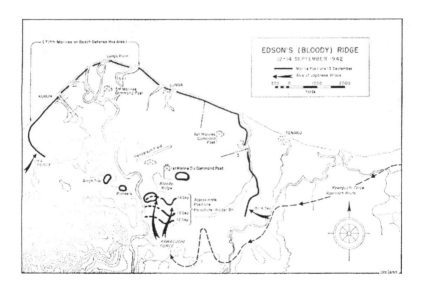

ADM. McCain visited Guadalcanal at the end of August. He arrived in time to greet the aerial reinforcements he had ordered, just in time for a taste of the Japanese nightly bombings. He got first-hand experience of another unwanted feature of the Cactus Air Force nights: being bombarded by

Japanese cruisers and destroyers. Gen. Vandegrift noted that Adm. McCain had gotten a dose of the "normal ration of shells." The admiral had seen enough and signaled his superiors; it was time to increase support for the Guadalcanal Operations.

He noted that it was "imperative and that the situation admits no delay whatsoever." He sent another message to admirals Nimitz and King:

Cactus can be a sinkhole for enemy air power and must be consolidated, expanded, and exploited to the enemy's mortal hurt.

On September 3, the commanding general of the 1st Marine Aircraft Wing, Gen. Roy Geiger, and his assistant wing commander, Col. Woods, moved forward into Guadalcanal and took charge of the air operations. These veteran Marine aviators signaled an instant lift to the morale of the pilots and ground crews. It reinforced the belief that they were on the leading edge of air combat, they were now setting the pace for the rest of Marine Corps aviation. Gen. Vandegrift could turn over the day-to-day management of the aerial defenses of Cactus to the able and experienced Gen. Geiger. There was no shortage of targets for the mixed air force of Marine, Navy, and Army flyers. Daily attacks by the Japanese, coupled with steady reinforcement attempts by enemy destroyers and transports, meant that every type of plane would lift off of the Henderson runway and was airborne as often as possible. The Seabees had begun work on a second airstrip, Fighter One, which would relieve most of the pressure of the primary airfield.

By now, most of Gen. Kawaguchi's troops had reached Guadalcanal. Those who hadn't, missed landfall forever because of the American air assaults. Kawaguchi gambled with a surprise attack on the heart of the Marines' position. He planned a thrust from the jungle directly to the airfield. To reach his jump-off position, Kawaguchi would have to move through rugged terrain unobserved, carving his way through the dense vegetation and out of sight of the Marine patrols. This strenuous approach route would lead them into a prominent ridge topped by Kunai Grass that wove snakelike through the jungle to within a mile of the Henderson runway. Unknown to Japanese intelligence, Vandegrift Moved his HQ to a sheltered spot toward the inland base of the ridge, a better-protected site from enemy bombing and shell fire.

The success of the Japanese general's plan depended on the Marines keeping that inland perimeter thinly manned. They concentrated their forces on the west and east flanks. This would not happen. All available intelligence, including captured enemy maps, pointed to the likelihood of an attack on the airfield. Vandegrift moved his combined Parachute/Raider Battalion to the most apparent enemy approach throughout the ridge.

Col. Edson's men scouted Savo Island after moving into Guadalcanal and destroyed a Japanese supply base at Tasimboko. Another shorter raid took up positions on the forward slopes of the ridge at the edge of the encroaching jungle on September 10. Their commander said that he was convinced they were in the path of the next Japanese attack. The earlier patrols had spotted a sizable Japanese assault force approaching. Col. Edson patrolled extensively as his men dug in on the ridge. In the flanking jungle, Marines contacted enemy patrols who confirmed that Japanese troops were out front. Kawaguchi had two thousand of his men with him; enough, he thought, to punch through into the airfield.

Japanese bombers had dropped five-hundred-pound bombs along the ridge on the 11th, and enemy ships began showering the area after nightfall on the 12th, once the threat of American air attacks subsided. The first Japanese thrust came at 2100 against Col. Edson's left flank. They boiled out of the jungle, the enemy soldiers attacked fearlessly into the face of machine gun and rifle fire. They closed into bayonet range. The Marines pushed them back. Then they came on again—a coordinated attack against the right flank—and penetrated the Marines' positions. They were forced back again. A third attack ended the night's action, it was a close fight, but by 0230, Col. Edson told Vandegrift his men could hold. And they did.

On the morning of September 13, Col. Edson called his company commanders together and told them:

They were just testing, just testing. They will be back.

All defenses were ordered merged, and positions improved. He pulled his lines toward the airfield along the center spine of the ridge. The 2/5 Marines, were back up on Tulagi. They were moved into position to reinforce him again.

The following night's assaults were as fierce as any Marine had yet to see. The Japanese fought hand-to-hand everywhere. They were in the Marines' foxholes and gun pits, and streaming past positions to attack from the rear. Sgt. Major Banta shot one in the command post. Col. Edson appeared wherever the fighting was the toughest, encouraging his men to their utmost efforts. The hand-to-hand battles spilled out into the jungle on both flanks of the ridge. Engineer positions were attacked. The 5th Marine reserves were ordered into the fight. Artillery from the 5/11 Marines fired 105mm howitzers at called out targets. The range became as short as fifteen hundred yards from tube to impact.

The Japanese could stand no more. They pulled back at dawn. On the slopes of the ridge in the surrounding jungle, they left over seven hundred bodies, with another five hundred men wounded. The remnants of the Kawaguchi force staggered back toward their lines to the west. A grueling, hellish eight-day march that killed most of the enemy.

The cost to Col. Edson's force for its epic defense was also heavy. He lost fifty-nine men, ten missing in action, and nearly two hundred wounded. Coupled with the casualties and losses of Tulagi, Gavutu, and Tanambogo, this signaled the end of the 1st Parachute Battalion as an effective fighting force. Less than ninety men of the parachutists' original strength could walk off the ridge soon to be known as Bloody Ridge or Edson's Ridge. Due to his inspirational and heroic actions, Col. Edson was awarded the Medal of Honor.

Over the next two days, the Japanese attempted to support Kawaguchi's attack on the ridge against the flanks of the Marine perimeter. In the east, enemy troops tried to penetrate the lines of the 3rd Battalion, 1st Marines. Artillery fire caught them out in the open on the grass plane, causing over two hundred dead. To the west, the 3rd Battalion, 5th Marines continued to hold ridge positions that covered the coastal road and heroically fought off a determined Japanese attack force that skirmished its front lines.

7TH MARINES REINFORCE THE BATTALION

THE VICTORY at Col. Edson's Bloody Ridge boosted the Allied home front morale. It reinforced the idea, for the men ashore on Guadalcanal, that they could take out anything the enemy could send up against them. At higher levels of military command, the leaders were unsure if the ground Marines and their motley air force could hold out against the Japanese forces.

Captured Japanese dispatches uncovered the myth of the two thousand man sized defending force. The Imperial Japanese sent a sizable naval force and two divisions of Japanese troops to engage and conquer the Americans on Guadalcanal. The Cactus Air Force, boosted by Navy carrier squadrons, made the planned reinforcement a high-risk venture. This was a risk the Japanese were prepared to take.

On September 18, the long-awaited 7th Marines, reinforced the 1st Battalion, 11th Marines, and other division troops. When the men from Samoa landed, they were greeted with open arms by the Marines already on the island. The 7th had been the 1st regiment of the 1st Division to go overseas. Its men, many thought then, were likely the first Marines to see combat. The division had sent some of the best Marines to

Samoa, but now they had returned. A salty combat veteran of the 5th Marines said to a friend in the 7th that he was tired of waiting "to see our first team get into the game." A separate supply convoy reached the island at the same time as the 7th's arrival, bringing with it the first resupply of ammunition and aviation fuel since D-Day.

The naval force covering for the supply and reinforcement convoys was attacked by Japanese submarines. The battleship *North Carolina* was damaged and the carrier *Wasp* was torpedoed and sunk. The destroyer *O'Brien* was hit so severely, she broke up and sank on her way to drydock. The Navy accomplished the mission. The 7th Marines were landed, but with a terrible loss of life. One of the few optimistic outcomes of the devastating Japanese torpedo attack was the remainder of the *Wasp's* aircraft joined the cactus Air Force. Similar to what the planes of the *Enterprise* and *Saratoga* had done with their carriers. This left the *Hornet* as the only whole fleet carrier in the South Pacific.

As the ships that brought in the 7th Marines withdrew, they took with them the survivors of the 1st Parachute Battalion with sick bays full of badly wounded men. Gen. Vandegrift now had control over five artillery battalions, one under strength raider battalion, and ten battalions of infantry. The 3/2 Marines, arrived from Tulagi. The defensive perimeter was reorganized into ten sectors. He gave the engineer, pioneer, and amphibian tractor battalions sectors along the beach. The other sectors were manned by the infantry battalions, which included the jungle's inland perimeter. Each infantry regiment was assigned to battalions, one to be kept in reserve and one battalion online.

Gen. Vandegrift had a select group of infantrymen training to be scouts and snipers under Col. "Wild Bill" Whaling. An experienced jungle fighter, marksman, and hunter, he was appointed to run a school to sharpen the divisions' fighting skills. As the men finished their training under Col.

Whaling and went back to their outfits, others took their place and were available to scout and spearhead operations.

Now that Gen. Vandegrift had over nineteen thousand men onshore. He planned to take a forward position on the east bank of the Matanikau River. He probed the Japanese reaction with a strong force of Marines. Gen. Vandegrift chose the fresh 1st Battalion, 7th Marines, commanded by Lieut. Col. Lewis "Chesty" Puller, to move inland along the slopes of Mount Austin and to patrol north toward the coast and the Japanese held area.

Puller's battalion ran into Japanese troops bivouacked on the slopes of Mount Austin on the 24th and, in a sharp firefight, lost seven men and twenty-five wounded. Vandegrift had sent the 2/5 Marines, to reinforce Puller and help carry wounded men out of the jungle. Puller advanced with reinforcements moving along the east bank of the Matanikau River. He reached the coast on September 26 as planned. He encountered intense fire from ridges west of the river. He attempted to cross with the 2/5 Marines but was beaten back.

The 1st Raider Battalion was ordered to attack on the 27th and establish a patrol base west of the Matanikau River before they were sent inland to outflank the Japanese. The battalion, now commanded by Edson's former XO, Lieut. Col. Samuel Griffith, ran into a hornet's nest of Japanese who had crossed the Matanikau River during the night. A garbled message led Col. Edson to believe that Griffith's men were advancing according to the plan. He landed companies of the 1/7 Marines behind the Matanikau River and struck the Japanese from the rear. Another assault was launched across the river.

This landing was made without incident, and the 7th Marines moved inland only to be cut off and ambushed by the Japanese. A rescue force was ordered to assist. They moved with difficulty through Japanese fire and landing craft. The Marines evacuated after a tough fight under covering fire from a destroyer and machine guns of an overhead SBD. The 7th Marines returned to the perimeter, landing near Kukum. The Raider, and 5th Marines Battalions pulled back from the Matanikau. The Japanese strongly contested any westward advance, and it cost the Marines sixty men killed and over one hundred wounded.

The Japanese soldiers who the Marines had encountered were men from the 4th Regiment of the 2nd (*Sendai*) Division. Prisoners confirmed that the division was landing on the island. This included the enemy's reinforcement of 105mm howitzers, guns capable of shelling the airfield from positions as far out as Kokumbona. This was direct evidence of a new and more potent enemy attack.

September drew to a close, and several of the senior officers, picked in the order of when they joined the division, were sent back to the states. They would provide training and organization at a new level of combat expertise with the several new Marine Corps units now forming. The air wing was not ready to return its experienced pilots to the rear. The vital combat knowledge they possessed was needed in the training pipeline. But they, the survivors, would soon rotate back to the rear, some for a much needed R&R before returning to combat and others to lead new squadrons into the fight.

JAPANESE OFFENSIVE ON MARUYAMA TRAIL

On September 30, a B-17 carrying Adm. Nimitz made an emergency landing on Henderson Airfield. The admiral made the most of the opportunity. He took a tour of the front lines, saw Edson's Bloody Ridge, and spoke to several Marines. He reaffirmed to Gen. Vandegrift that the overriding mission was to hold the airfield. He awarded Navy Crosses to several Marines, including Gen. Vandegrift, and promised all the support he could give. He left the next day visibly encouraged by what he had seen.

The next Marine assault involved a punishing return to Matanikau. Whaling commanded five infantry battalions along with his men in the 3/2 Marines. He surged inland, clearing the way for the 7th Marines. Their objective was to drive through and hook toward the coast, destroying the Japanese along the Matanikau. Col. Hudson's 2nd and 3rd Battalions were set to attack across the river's mouth. The rest of the division's artillery was positioned to fire in the support role.

Whaling's force moved into the jungle upstream of the Matanikau. They encountered Japanese troops that harassed his forward elements, but not in enough strength to stop the advance. He bypassed the enemy and dug in for the night. Behind him was the 7th Marines, prepared to move through the lines, cross the river, and attack north toward the Japanese. The 5th Marines Assault Battalion moved toward the Matanikau. They ran into the Japanese in strength less than four hundred yards from the river.

They had run into a strong advance element of the Japanese 4th Regiment, which had crossed the Matanikau to set up a base from which they could fire artillery into the Marine perimeter. The fighting was intense. Even though the 2nd Battalion encountered little opposition and broke through to the riverbank, they turned north. They hit the inland flank of the enemy troops. Gen. Vandegrift sent a company of raiders forward to reinforce the 5th and maintain a holding position toward the beach.

On October 8, rain poured all day long, stopping virtually all forward progress. It did not stop the hand-to-hand fighting around the pockets of Japanese. When the enemy troops retreated, they attempted to escape the encircling Marines. They smashed into the raiders' position near their escape route. Wild hand-to-hand combat ensued, and only a few Japanese broke through to reach across the river. The rest died fighting.

The next day, Whaling's force, flanked by the 2nd and the 1/7 Marines, crossed the Matanikau. They turned and continued to follow ridgelines to the sea. Puller's battalion discovered several Japanese in a ravine to his front, fired his mortars, and called in artillery. His men used rifles and machine guns to pick off enemy troops trying to escape. When his ammunition ran short, Puller pushed inland toward the beach to link up with Whaling's force, which had encountered no opposition. The Marines then recrossed the Matanikau River, joined Col. Edson's troops, and marched back to the perimeter. They left a strong combat outpost at the Matanikau now clear of Japanese. Vandegrift, informed by intelligent sources that a major Japanese attack was coming from the west, consolidated his positions.

He left no sizable Marine force more than a day's march from the perimeter. The Marine advance on October 8 had thwarted the Japanese plans for an early attack and cost the enemy over seven hundred dead. The Marines paid a hefty price as well, 65 killed and 130 wounded.

Disease was killing men in numbers equal to the battle casualties. Crippling stomach cramps known as gastroenteritis and other tropical fungus infections like "jungle rot," infamous for uncomfortable rashes on men's armpits, elbows, feet, and crotches—a product of seldom being dry. If it didn't rain, sweat provided moisture. Along with this came hundreds of malaria cases. Atabrine tablets were some relief. Besides turning the skin yellow, they were not effective enough to stop the spread of the mosquito-borne infection. Malaria attacks were becoming so severe that nothing short of complete prostration, becoming a litter case, could earn a rest in the hospital. These diseases affected the men who had been on the island the longest, especially those who experienced the early days with short rations. Gen. Vandegrift suggested that when his men got relieved, they should not be sent to another tropical island hospital. But to a place where a genuine change of atmosphere and climate existed. He asked for Wellington or Auckland in New Zealand to be considered.

Under present circumstances, there was no relief for the men starting their third month on Guadalcanal. The Japanese did not abandon their plan to seize back Guadalcanal and gave painful evidence of their intentions in mid-October. General Hyakutake landed on Guadalcanal to oversee the Imperial Japanese offensive. The elements of Gen. Maruyama's *Sendai* Division was already a factor in the fighting near the Matanikau River. More enemy troops were coming. The

Japanese were taking advantage that the Cactus Air Force flyers had no night attack capability. They planned to ensure that no planes at all would rise from Guadalcanal to meet them.

On October 11, US Navy surface ships assisted in stopping the "Tokyo Express." The nickname given to Adm. Tanaka's almost nightly reinforcement for his covering force of five cruisers and destroyers. Adm. Scott, who commanded Renell Island, got word enemy ships were approaching Guadalcanal.

Adm. Scott's mission was to protect an approaching reinforcement convoy. He steamed at flank speed eager to engage the enemy. He encountered more ships than expected, three heavy cruisers and two destroyers, as well as six destroyers escorting two seaplane carrier transports. Adm. Scott maneuvered between Cape Esperance and Savo Island—Guadalcanal's western tip. He engaged the bombardment group head-on.

Alerted from the scout plane on his flagship, *San Francisco*, the spotting's later confirmed by radar on the *Helena*. The Americans could open fire first because the Japanese had no radar and did not know of their presence. When the Japanese enemy destroyer sank immediately, two cruisers were severely damaged. Another remaining cruiser and destroyer turned away from the hellish inferno of American fire. Adm. Scott's own force was punished by enemy fire, which damaged two cruisers and two destroyers, one of which, the *Duncan*, sank the next day. The Cactus Air Force flyers spotted two reinforcement destroyer escorts retreating and sank them both. Named The Battle of Cape Esperance, it would be counted as an American naval victory—one sorely needed.

A welcome reinforcement convoy arrived on the island on October 13 when the 164th Infantry Regiment of the newly formed Americal Division arrived. These soldiers were members of a National Guard outfit from North Dakota. They were equipped with Garand M1 rifles—a weapon most overseas Marines had only heard of. The rate of fire of the semi-automatic Garand outperformed the single shot, bolt action Springfield's that the Marines carried, and the bolt action rifles carried by the Japanese. Most 1st Division Marines believed their Springfield's were more accurate and a better weapon. This did not stop some light-fingered Marines from acquiring these new weapons when the occasion presented itself. Such an opportunity arose when the soldiers were landing, and supplies were being moved to the dumps.

Flights of Japanese bombers appeared over Henderson Field, unscathed by the defending fighters, and started dropping bombs. The soldiers headed for cover, and the alert Marines inured to the bombing, used this interval to "liberate" interesting crates and cartons. The news that the Army had arrived spread across the island like wildfire. There was hope. It meant the Marines may eventually be relieved.

If the bombing wasn't enough grief, the Japanese opened on the airfield with their 150mm howitzers. The men of the 164th, commanded by Col. Robert Hall, got a rude welcome to Guadalcanal. On that night, October 13, they shared a terrifying experience with the Marines that no one would ever forget.

The Imperial Japanese were determined to knock out Henderson Field to protect their soldiers landing in strength west of Koli Point. The enemy commander sent the battleships *Kongo* and *Haruna* into Ironbottom Sound to bombard the Marine positions. The Japanese flare planes signaled the bombardment, seventy-five minutes of sheer hell, 14-inch shells exploding with such a devastating effect that even cruiser fire was barely noticed.

No place was safe. No one was safe. No dugout could withstand the fury of 14-inch shells. One seasoned veteran used to being cool under enemy fire said nothing was worse in war than being helpless on the receiving end of naval gunfire. "Huge trees being cut apart and flying about like toothpicks," he said.

The airfield and surrounding area were reduced to a fiery shambles when dawn broke. The naval shelling, and artillery fire and bombing left the Cactus Air Force commander, Gen. Geiger, with only a handful of aircraft still operational. Henderson Airfield was now thickly cratered with shells and bombs, and a death toll of forty-one. The Cactus Air Force flyers had to attack because the morning revealed a shore and sea full of inviting targets.

Japanese transports and landing craft had broken through. The enemy was now everywhere near Tassafaronga. The escorting cruisers and destroyers had proven to be a formidable screen of antiaircraft. Every American plane that could fly was in the fight. Gen. Geiger's aid, Maj. Jack Cram, took off, in the generals PBY, rigged with two torpedoes. He put one into the side of an enemy transport as it unloaded. A new squadron of F4Fs took part in the day's action. He landed, refueled, and took off again to join in the fight. After an hour, when he landed again, he had four enemy bomber kills. Bauer, had over twenty Japanese aircraft kills and in later air battles, was killed in action. He was posthumously awarded the Medal of Honor along with four other Marine pilots in the early days of the Cactus Air Force.

General Hyakutake believed the Japanese had now landed enough troops to destroy the Marines occupied beachhead and seize the airfield. He approved General Maruyama's

ON

objective to move most of the *Sendai* Division out of sight through the jungle without engaging the Marines. They were to strike south near Edson's Ridge. With seven thousand men, each carrying a mortar or artillery shell, they trekked along the Maruyama Trail. General Maruyama had approved the trail's name to show his deep confidence. He intended to support this attack with infantry guns and heavy mortars—70mm pack howitzers. The men had to push, lug, and drag the supporting guns over miles of broken ground, two major streams, the Matanikau and the Lunga, and through heavy underbrush, for their commander's path to glory.

Gen. Vandegrift knew the Japanese were going to attack. Patrols and reconnaissance flights had shown the push would come from the west, where the enemy reinforcements had landed. The American commander changed his disposition. There were now Japanese troops east of the perimeter, but not in any considerable strength. The 164th Infantry Regiment, reinforced by the Marine Special Weapons Unit, was put into the fight to hold the sixty-six-hundred-yard eastern flank.

They curved inland to meet up with the 7th Marines near Edson's Ridge. The 7th Marines held twenty-five-hundred-yards of the ridge to the Lunga. From the Lunga, the 1st Marines had a thirty-five-hundred-yard sector of jungle which ran west to the point of the line curving back again toward the beach in the 5th Marines' sector. Since the attack was expected from the west, the 3rd Battalion's Marines kept a strong outpost position forward of the 1st Marines' lines along the east bank of the Matanikau.

In the lull before the attack—if Japanese destroyer cruiser bombardments, artillery harassment, and bomber attacks could be called a lull—Gen. Vandegrift was visited by the commandant of the Marine Corps, Lieut. Gen. Thomas Holcomb. The commandant flew in on October 21 to see for himself how the Marines were faring. It proved to be an occasion for both senior Marines to meet the new commander of the South Pacific, Adm. "Bull" Halsey. Adm. Nimitz had announced Halsey's appointment on October 18. The news was welcome in the Marine and Navy ranks throughout the Pacific.

Halsey's well-deserved reputation for aggressiveness promised renewed attention to the situation on Guadalcanal. On the 22nd, Holcomb and Vandegrift flew to Noumea to meet with Halsey. They gave a round of briefings about the Allied situation. After Vandegrift described his position, he argued against the diversion of reinforcements intended for the Cactus Air Force to any other South Pacific venue. He argued that he needed all of the Americal Division and another two Marine Division regiments to beef up his forces. He also said that more than half of his veterans were worn out by over three months of fighting the ravages of jungle incurred diseases. Adm. Halsey told the Marine Corps general:

You go back there, Vandegrift. I promise to get you everything I have.

When Gen. Vandegrift returned to Guadalcanal, Adm. Holcomb moved on to Pearl Harbor to meet with Adm. Nimitz. He brought with him Halsey's recommendation that, landing force commanders, once established onshore, would have equal command status with Navy amphibious force commanders. At Pearl Harbor, Adm. Nimitz approved Halsey's recommendations as well as in Washington. This meant that the command status of all future Pacific amphibious operations was determined by the events of Guadalcanal.

Another piece of news Vandegrift received from Holcomb, was that if Pres. Roosevelt did not reappoint him, (which was likely because of his age), he would recommend that Vandegrift be appointed as the next Commandant of the Marine Corps. This news did not divert Vandegrift's attention when he flew back to Guadalcanal. The Japanese were in the middle of their offensive. An enemy patrol accompanied by two tanks on the twentieth tried to find a way through the line held by the 3/1 Marines. A sharpshooting 37mm gun crew knocked out a lead tank, and the enemy's force fell back. In the meantime shelling the Marines' positions with artillery.

On sunset the next day, the Japanese tried again, this time with more artillery fire and more tanks in the fray. But again, a 37mm gun knocked out the lead tank and discouraged the attack. On October 22, the enemy paused, waiting for General Maruyama's force to get inland. The 23rd was planned as the day of the main Japanese assault. They dropped a heavy rain of artillery and mortar fire on Marine positions near the Matanikau River mouth. At dusk, nine 18 ton medium tanks clanked out of the trees onto the river sandbar. Eight of them were peppered by the 37mm. One tank made it across the river, a Marine blasted its track off with a grenade, and a 75mm half-track was destroyed in the ocean surf. The remaining enemy infantry was annihilated by Marine artillery fire. Hundreds of Japanese casualties and three more tanks were destroyed. A later inland thrust further upstream was beaten back. The coastal attack did nothing to General Maruyama's island offensive. This caused Vandegrift to move one battalion, the 2nd Battalion, 7th Marines, into the four-thousand-yard gap between the Matanikau perimeter and position. This move proved helpful since one of General Maruyama's attacks was headed directly to this area.

Although patrols had encountered no Japanese south or east of the jungle perimeter up to the 24th, these attempts had alerted everyone. Gen. Maruyama was satisfied his men had struggled to gain the appropriate assault positions after delaying the attack for thirty-three days. He began his assault on October 24, but the Marines were waiting. An observer spotted an enemy officer surveying Edson's Ridge on the 24th. Scout snipers reported smoke from rice fires rising from the valley two miles south of "Chesty" Puller's positions. Six battalions of the Japanese *Sendai* Division were poised to attack. Near midnight, the first elements of the enemy hit and bypassed a platoon-sized outpost forward of Puller's barbed wire entanglements. Puller's men waited, straining to see through the dark night in the driving rain. When the Japanese charged out of the jungle attacking Puller's area near the ridge in the flat ground to the east, the Marines reacted with every-thing they had. They called in artillery, fired mortars, and relied heavily on crossing fields of machine gun fire to cut down enemy infantrymen. Japanese mortars, artillery, and other supporting armaments were thrown back along the Maruyama Trail. They had proved too much of a burden for the infantrymen to carry.

This drove a wedge into the Marine lines. But everything straightened out with repeated counterattacks. Puller realized his battalion was being hit by a strong Japanese force capable of repeated attacks. He requested reinforcements. The Army's 3rd Battalion, 164th Infantry, was ordered to move forward. Men slipped and slid in the rain as they trudged a mile south along Edson's Ridge. Puller met Col. Robert Hall at the head of the column, and they walked down the length of the Marine lines peeling off Army squads one at a time to feed into the lines. The enemy attacked again throughout the night. Marines and soldiers fought back together.

By 0330, the Army battalion was completely assimilated into the 1/7 Marines' lines, and the enemy attacks were getting weaker. The Americans returned fire. They used flanking fire from machine guns and the 37mm guns remaining in the positions held by the 2nd Battalion and

164th Infantry on Puller's left. Near dawn, Gen. Maruyama pulled his men back to regroup and prepare to attack again.

At daylight, Puller and Hall reordered the lines. They put the 2nd Battalion and the 164th into their own positions on Puller's left flank. The driving rains had turned Henderson Field into a quagmire. This grounded the Cactus Air Force flyers. Japanese planes used this "free ride" to bomb Marine positions. Enemy artillery fire continued along with a pair of Japanese destroyers adding in on the bombardment until they got too close to shore. The 3rd defense Battalion's 5-inch guns repelled them. As the sun rose, the runways dried and afternoon enemy attacks were now met by the Cactus Air Force fighters—who downed twenty-two Japanese planes with only a loss of three.

As night came on again, Gen. Maruyama tried more of the same with the same result. The Marine/Army lines held, and the Japanese were cut down in droves by rifle, mortar, machine gun, 37mm, and artillery fire from the west. The Japanese mounted three attacks on positions held by the 2/7 Marines. The enemy broke through the positions held by Company F. Still, a counter-attack led by the battalion's XO drove off the Japanese again at daylight. The American positions were secured, and the enemy had retreated. They would not return. The Imperial Japanese offensive using the *Sendai* Division was defeated.

Over thirty-five hundred Imperial Japanese troops died during these attacks. General Maruyama's boast that he would "exterminate the enemy Americans around the airfield in one blow" had proven empty. The remainder of his force now limped back over the Maruyama Trail, with mostly wounded men. The soldiers and Marines, together, lost just under three hundred men killed and wounded.

The existing records are sketchy and incomplete. One

result of the battle was a warm welcome to the 164th Infantry from the 1st Marine Division. Vandegrift commended Col. Hall's battalion and said:

The division was proud to have serving with it another unit which had stood the test of battle.

Through the heroics of two nights of constant brutal fighting, several Marines were singled out for recognition. Two outstanding Marines were Sgt. John Basilone of the 1/7 Marines, and Sgt. Mitchell Paige of the 2nd Battalion. Both of these Marines were machine gun section leads recognized as having performed above and beyond the call of duty in the inspiring words of their Medal of Honor citations.

FIGHTING WITHDRAWAL ALONG THE BEACH

WHILE THE MARINES and soldiers battled the Japanese ashore, A patrol plane sighted a sizeable Japanese fleet near the Santa Cruz Islands, east of the Solomons. The enemy force was formidable for battleships and for carriers with twenty-eight destroyers and eight cruisers. Adm. Halsey was poised for a victorious attack after the capture of Henderson Field. He signaled Adm. Kincaid, with the *Hornet* and *Enterprise* carrier groups, and ordered them to attack.

On October 26, American planes located the Japanese carriers. The Japanese *Zuiho*'s flight deck was damaged by the scout bombers, canceling their flight operations. But three other carriers launched strikes. A dogfight raged overhead as each side's planes strove to reach the other's carriers. The *Hornet* was hit repeatedly by torpedoes and bombs. Two Japanese pilots crashed their planes into the deck. The damage to the ship was so massive, the *Hornet* was abandoned and sunk. The *Enterprise*, the battleship *South Dakota*, the light cruiser *San Juan*, and the destroyer *Smith* were also hit. The destroyer *Porter* was sunk. On the Japanese side—no ships were sunk. Three carriers and two destroyers were damaged. One hundred Japanese planes were lost. Seventy-five US planes went down. This was considered a standoff. The Imperial Japanese Navy could have continued their attacks but were discouraged by the defeat of their ground forces and withdrew to attack another day.

The enemy naval force departure marked a period in which sizable reinforcements reached the island. The 2nd Marines' headquarters found transport space to come up from Espiritu Santo on October 29. Col. Arthur moved his regiment from Tulagi to Guadalcanal, changing out the 1st and 2nd Battalions for the well bloodied 3rd Division, which took up the Tulagi duties. The 2nd Marines' battalions at Tulagi had performed the task of scouting and securing all the small islands of the Florida group. They were frustrated, only being able to watch the battles taking place across the Sealark Channel. These Marines could now take part in the big show.

US planes flew into the Cactus fields from the island of New Caledonia. Squadrons of MAG-11 fighters moved forward from New Caledonia to Espiritu Santo to be closer to the battle. The flight echelons could now operate forward to Guadalcanal with relative ease. Two batteries of 155mm guns landed on November 2, providing Vandegrift with his first artillery units capable of matching the enemy's long-range 150mm guns. The 8th Marines had arrived from American Samoa. The full-strength regiment, reinforced by the 75mm howitzers of the 1st Battalion, 10th Marines, added another four thousand men to the defending forces. These fresh troops reflected a renewed emphasis at all levels of command, ensuring that Guadalcanal would hold no matter the cost. The reinforcement/replacement pipeline was being filled. The rest of the 2nd Marine Division, and the Army's 25th Infantry Division arrived. More planes of every type from American as well as Allied sources were slated to reinforce and replace the battle-weary Cactus Air Force veterans.

The increased pace of reinforcement was provided by Pres. Roosevelt. Cutting through the demands for American forces worldwide, he told each of the Joint Chiefs, on October 24, that Guadalcanal must be reinforced immediately. The operational pace on Guadalcanal did not slacken after the Japanese offensive was pushed back. Gen. Vandegrift wanted to clear the area immediately west of the Matanikau of all troops, forestalling another buildup of attacking forces. Adm. Tanaka's Tokyo express was still operating despite punishing attacks by the Cactus aircraft and American motor torpedo boats now based at Tulagi.

On November 1-5, Marines backed up by the newly arrived 2nd Marines, attacked across bridges engineers had laid over the Matanikau River the previous night. Inland, Col. Whaling led his scout snipers in a screening movement with the main driving attack to protect the flank. The opposition was fierce in the shore area where they drove forward toward Point Cruz, but Whaling's group encountered little resistance. At nightfall, when the Marines dug in, the only sizable enemy force was in the Point Cruz area. In the days of bitter fighting, Cpl. Anthony Casamento, a badly wounded machine gun squad leader in Edson's 1st Battalion, distinguished himself so well that he was recommended for a Navy Cross. Many years later, in August 1980, Pres. Jimmy Carter approved the award for the Medal of Honor in its stead.

The attack continued with the reserve 3rd Battalion moving into the fight and all 3/5 Marine units moving to surround enemy defenders. On November 3, the Japanese pocket just west of the base at Point Cruz was eliminated. Well over three hundred enemy soldiers had been killed. The Marines encountered light resistance and slowly advanced across the rugged terrain one thousand yards beyond the 5th Marines' action.

The offensive objectives seemed well in hand, and the advance halted. Intelligence was reported that a substantial enemy reinforcement attempt was underway. Gen. Vandegrift pulled most of his men back to safeguard the perimeter of the airfield. This time he left a regiment to outpost the ground that had been gained. Col. Arthur's 2nd Marines reinforced the Army's 164th Infantry.

Gen. Vandegrift emphasized the need to be cautious because the Japanese were again discovered in strength, east of the perimeter. On November 3, Lieut. Col. Hanneken's 2/7 Marines on a reconnaissance in force toward Koli Point, could see the Japanese ships clustered, eight miles from the perimeter. His men encountered strong Japanese resistance from fresh troops, and he pulled back. A regiment of the enemy's 38th Division landed as Hyakutake used the Japanese Navy to attack the perimeter from both flanks.

Hanneken's battalion executed a fighting withdrawal along the beach. They took fire from the jungle inland. A rescue force was soon put together comprised of two tank companies, the 1/7 Marines, and the 2nd and 3rd Battalions of the 164th Infantry. The Japanese troops, members of the 38th Division Regiment and remnants of Kawaguchi's brigade, fought to hold ground as the US Marines and Army drove forward along the coast. Marines and soldiers attempted to outflank the enemy in the jungle. This battle lasted for days, supported by Cactus Air, naval gunfire, and the newly landed 155mm guns.

The Japanese commander received new orders as he struggled to hold back the Americans. He was to move inland and break off the action in March to rejoin the main Japanese forces west of the perimeter—a tall order to fill. This two-pronged attack had been abandoned. The Japanese managed the 1st part. Japanese soldiers found a gap in the 164th line and broke through along a meandering jungle stream. They left 450 dead throughout a seven-day battle. The Army and the Marines had lost forty dead in one hundred and twenty-five wounded. The enemy soldiers who broke out from the encircling Americans escaped into worse circumstances.

Adm. Turner had employed one of his several plans for

alternate landings and beachheads. All of which Gen. Vande-grift opposed. At Aola Bay, forty miles east of the main perimeter, the Navy put an airfield construction and defense force ashore on November 4. While the Japanese were still battling Marines near Tetere, Vandegrift persuaded Turner to detach part of his landing force, the 2nd Raider Battalion, to sweep west and destroy any enemy forces it encountered.

Col. Carlson's Raider Battalion had already seen action before reaching Guadalcanal. An additional two companies had reinforced the Midway Island offenders when the Japanese attacked in June. The remainder of the battalion landed on the Macon Islands and destroyed the garrison. For his part in the fighting, Sgt. Clyde Thomason was awarded a Medal of Honor, the first Marine enlisted to receive his country's highest award in World War II.

Marching from Aola Bay, The 2nd Raider Battalion encountered the Japanese attempting to retreat to the west. On November 12, the raiders beat off attacks by two enemy companies. They pursued the Japanese, fighting a series of small actions over the next five days before making contact with the main Japanese force. For two weeks, the raiders came down from the jungle ridges into the perimeter, harassing the retreating enemy. They killed over five hundred Japanese soldiers. Their losses were only sixteen dead and eighteen wounded. This mission at Aola Bay provided the 2nd Raider Battalion a starting point for its month-long jungle campaign but proved to be a bust. The site chosen for an airfield was unacceptable—too wet and unstable. The entire force moved to Koli Point in early December, where another airfield was constructed.

The build-up on Guadalcanal continued. On November 11, guarded by a destroyer/cruiser covering force, a convoy was attacked by enemy bombers. Three transports were hit, but the men still landed. These men were badly needed. Gen. Vandegrift's veterans on Guadalcanal were ready to be replaced.

Malaria cases were averaging over one thousand a week besides related diseases. Enemy soldiers who had been on the island for any length of time were in no better shape. Rations and medical supplies were scarce. The entire thrust of the Japanese reinforcement effort continued to get troops and combat equipment ashore. In Tokyo, the idea prevailed that despite all evidence to the contrary, one overwhelming coordinated assault would crush the American resistance. The enemy drive to take Port Moresby, New Guinea, was put on hold to put all of their effort into driving the Americans off Guadalcanal.

On November 12, Japanese naval forces converged on Guadalcanal to cover the landing of the main body of the 38th Division. Adm. Callahan's cruisers and destroyers moved in to confront the enemy. Coastwatcher and scout plane sightings and radio intercepts identified two carriers, two battleships, four cruisers, and a host of destroyers heading toward Guadalcanal. The battleships were led by *Hiei* and *Kirishima* with the light cruiser *Nagura*, and fifteen destroyers spearheaded the bombardment and attack.

Just after midnight, Callahan's cruisers picked up the Japanese on radar and continue to close. The battle was fought at such a short-range that each side fired at their own ships. Callahan's flagship, *San Francisco*, was hit fifteen times. Callahan was killed; his ship limped away. The cruiser *Atlanta* was also hit and set ablaze. Adm. Scott, who was on board, was killed. Despite the hammering by the Japanese fire, the Americans held and continued fighting. The battleship *Hiei* was hit by over eighty shells. Badly damaged, it retired, and with it the rest of the attack force. Four destroyers were damaged, and three others were sunk. The Americans accomplished their purpose. They'd forced the Japanese to turn back. But the cost was high. Two antiaircraft cruisers, the *Juneau* and the *Atlanta*, were sunk. For destroyers, the *Laffey*, the *Monssen*, the *Cushing*, and the *Barton* also went to the bottom. The *San Francisco*, the heavy cruiser *Portland*, and the destroyers *Sterret* and *Aaron Ward* were also damaged. Only one destroyer of the thirteen American ships engaged, the *Fletcher*, was unscathed when survivors retired to the New Hebrides.

At dawn came the Cactus bombers and fighters. They attacked the crippled *Hiei* and pounded it ruthlessly. The Japanese were forced to scuttle her on the 14th. Adm. Halsey ordered his only surviving carrier, the *Enterprise*, out of Guadalcanal to get it out of reach of Japanese aircraft. He sent in his battleships the *South Dakota*, *Washington*, and escorting destroyers north to meet the Japanese. Some of the *Enterprise's* planes flew into Henderson Field to help even the odds.

On November 14, Cactus and *Enterprise* flyers found a Japanese destroyer/cruiser force that had pounded the island the night before. They damaged four cruisers and a destroyer. They quickly refueled and rearmed and went on the hunt for the approaching Japanese troop convoy. They hit several transports and sank one. Army B-17s from Espiritu Santo scored one hit and several near hits, bombing from over 17,000 feet. In a persistent pattern of attack, return, refuel, rearm, and resume, Guadalcanal planes hit nine transports— sinking seven. Many of the five thousand troops on the damaged ships were rescued by Tanaka's destroyers.

The Japanese fired furiously and laid smokescreens to protect the transports. General Tanaka later recalled:

Bomb's wobbling down from highflying B-17s, of carrier bombers roared toward targets as though to plunge full in the water, releasing bombs and pulling out barely in time; each miss

*sending up towering columns of mist and spray; every hit raising
clouds of smoke and fire.*

Despite the intensive attack, Tanaka continued on to Guadalcanal with four transports and four destroyers. Imperial Japanese intelligence learned of the oncoming American battleship force and rushed to warn Tanaka. Japanese admirals sent their own cruiser/battleship force to intercept. The Americans led by Adm. Lee on the *Washington*, reached the Sealark Channel by 2100 on the 14th. A Japanese cruiser was picked up north of Savo Island an hour later, and battleship fire repelled her. The Japanese now understood the opponents they expected would not be the cruisers. This clash, fought in the glare of gunfire and Japanese searchlights, was the most significant fight at sea for Guadalcanal. When the battle was over, the American battleships' 16-inch guns had more than matched the Japanese. Both *South Dakota* and *Washington* were damaged so severely they were forced to withdraw.

One Japanese and three American destroyers were sunk. When the Japanese attack force retired, Adm. Tanaka ran his four transports onto the beach. He knew they would be targets at daylight. Most men on board managed to get ashore before the expected pummeling by American warships, planes, and artillery. The Japanese had landed ten thousand troops of the 38th Division. But they were in no shape to ever again attempt a massive reinforcement. The horrific losses caused by the frequent naval clashes, which seemed to favor the Japanese, did not represent a standoff. Every American ship damaged or lost would be replaced. Every Japanese ship was precious to their steadily diminishing fleet. The air fighting losses on both sides were overwhelming. The Japanese would never recover from the loss of its experienced carrier pilots. In the Battle of the Philippine Sea between Japanese and American carriers, it would be called the "Mariana's Turkey Shoot" because of the ineptitude of the Japanese trainee pilots.

The enemy troops fortunate enough to reach land were not ready to assault the American positions. The 30th Division and the remnants of the various Japanese units attempting to penetrate the Marine lines needed to be trained in built into a coherent attack force before Gen. Hyakutake could have any reasonable attempt at taking Henderson Field. Gen. Vandegrift now had enough men and fresh units to replace his veteran troops along the front lines. He swapped the 1st Marine Division with the Army's 25th Infantry. Adm. Turner told Vandegrift to leave all of his heavy equipment on the island, and when he pulled out "in hopes of getting your units re-equipped when you come out."

He told Vandegrift that the Army would now command the final phases, since it would provide most combat forces once the 1st Division Marines departed. Maj. Gen. Alexander Patch, commander of the Americal Division, would relieve Vandegrift as senior American officer ashore. His air support would continue to be Marine dominated with Gen. Geiger, now on Espiritu Santo with 1st Wing headquarters fighter squadrons, to maintain the offensive. The Guadalcanal air command would be a mixture of Marine, Navy, Army, and Allied squadrons.

The sick list of the 1st Marine Division in November was over three thousand men with malaria. The men of the 1st Division still manned the frontline foxholes and rear areas, if any place within Guadalcanal's perimeter could properly be called a rear area. The men were exhausted. They had done their part of the fighting and they all knew it. On November 29, Gen. Vandegrift was handed a message from the Joint Chiefs of Staff. The crux of it read:

1st Marine Division is to be relieved without delay. And will proceed to Australia for rehabilitation and employment.

The word spread that the 1st Division was leaving and where it was going. Australia was not yet the special place it would become in the division's future, but anywhere was better than Guadalcanal.

DEFEAT OF JAPANESE FORCES ON GUADALCANAL

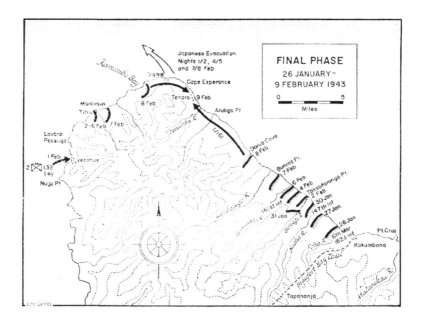

ON DECEMBER 7, one year after the Japanese assault on Pearl Harbor, Gen. Vandegrift sent a message to all under his command thanking them for their steadfastness and courage. He reminded them of their unbelievable achievements they'd made on Guadalcanal, now a synonym for disaster and death in the Japanese language. On December 9, he handed over his command to General Patch and flew out to Australia.

Elements of the 5th Marines boarded ship. The 1st, 11th, and 7th Marines soon followed together with the rest of the division's supporting units. The men that left with him were tired, thin, hollow-eyed, and demoralized.

This group of young men had grown considerably older in only four months. They left behind 681 dead Marines in the island cemetery. The final regiment of the 132nd Infantry of the American Division landed on December 8 as the 5th Marines prepared to leave. The 2nd Marine Division's regiments were already on the island. The 6th Marines were on their way to rejoin. Many of the men of the 2nd Marines, who landed on D-Day August 7, should have also left. They took little comfort in the thought that they, by all rights, should be the first of the 2nd Division to leave Guadalcanal whenever the day came.

A steady stream of replacements and ground reinforcements came to General Patch in December. He was still not ready to undertake a full-scale offensive until the 25th Division, and the rest of the 2nd Marine Division arrived. He kept all reconnaissance patrols and frontline units active—especially toward the western flank. The island commanders' air defense capabilities multiplied. The Cactus Air Force was organized into a fighter command and a strike and bomber command. They now operated from the newly redesignated Marine Corps airbase. Henderson Airfield had a new airstrip, Fighter Two. Fighter Two replaced Fighter One, which had suffered severe drainage problems.

Gen. Lewis Woods took over as senior aviator when Gen. Geiger returned to Espiritu Santo. Geiger was relieved on December 26 by Gen. Francis Mulcahy, the commanding

General of the 2nd Marine Aircraft Wing. New bomber and fighter squadrons were added regularly. The Army added a bomber squadron of B-26s. The Royal New Zealand Air Force flew in a reconnaissance squadron of Lockheed Hudsons. The US Navy sent a squadron of PBY Catalina patrol planes, with night-flying capability.

This aerial buildup forced the Imperial Japanese to curb air attacks and make their daylight naval reinforcement attempts an event of the past. The nighttime visits of the Tokyo Express destroyers now only brought supplies encased in metal drums rolled over the ship sides, hoping to float into shore. The men on shore desperately needed everything that could be sent, even by this method. But most of the drums never reached the beaches.

No matter how desperate the enemy situation was becoming, the Imperial Japanese were prepared to fight. General Hyakutake continued to plan the seizure of the airfield. He ordered the commander of the *Eighth Area Army* to continue the offensive. General Imamura had fifty thousand men to add and reinforce to the embattled Japanese troops on Guadalcanal.

Before the enemy units could be used, the Americans were prepared to move out from the perimeter on their own offensive. They knew that the Mt. Austin area was a continuing threat to their inland flank. Gen. Patch committed the Americal's 132nd Infantry to clearing the mountain's wooded slopes on December 17. The Army was successful in isolating the major Japanese force in the area by early January. The 1/2 Marines took uphill positions to the southeast of the 132nd to increase flank protection. By now, the 25th Infantry Division had arrived. So had the 6th Marines and the rest of the 2nd

Division's headquarters and support troops. Gen. De Carre took charge of all Marine ground forces on the island. The 2nd Division's commander Gen. John Marston remained in New Zealand because he was senior to General Patch.

General Patch was in command of three divisions and designated as the XIV Corps Commanding General on January 2. His Corps headquarters numbered less than twenty officers and men, almost all taken from Americal staff. Gen. Sebree, who had already led both Army and Marine units in attacks on the Japanese, took command of the Americal Division. On January 10, General Patch gave the signal to start the most vigorous American offensive in the Guadalcanal campaign. The mission of the troops was to attack and destroy remaining Japanese forces on Guadalcanal.

The objective of the Marine Corps attack was a line fifteen hundred yards west of the jump-off positions. These lines ran inland from Point Cruz to the vicinity of Hill 66— three thousand yards from the beach. To reach Hill 66, the 25th Infantry Division attacked with the 27th and 35th Infantry driving west and southwest across a scrambled series of ridges. The going was rough against a dug-in enemy. Elements of two regiments of the 38th Division gave way reluctantly and slowly. By the 13th, American soldiers aided by 1/2 Division Marines had won through two positions on the southern flank of the 2nd Marine Division.

On January 12, the Marines began their advance with the 8th Marines along the shore and 2nd Division Marines inland. At the base of Point Cruz in the 3/8 Marine sector, regimental weapons company half-tracks ran over half a dozen enemy machine gun nests. This attack was held up by an extensive emplacement unit. The weapons company commander, Capt. Henry Crow, took charge of the squad of Marine infantrymen taking cover from enemy fire with the classic line:

You'll never get a Purple Heart hiding in a foxhole. Follow me!

The men followed and destroyed the emplacement.

The going was difficult along the front of the advancing assault companies. The remnants of the Japanese *Sendai* Division were dug in on a series of cross compartments. Their fire took Marines in the flank advances. The progress was slow despite massive artillery support and naval gunfire from offshore destroyers. In over two days of heavy fighting, flamethrowers were used for the first time, and tanks were brought into play. The 2nd Division Marines were relieved, and the 6th Marines moved into the attack along the coast while the 8th Marines advanced inland. Naval gunfire spotted by officers onshore improved the accuracy. The Marines and Army reached their initial core objective on the 15th. In the attack zone, over six hundred Japanese had been killed.

The battle-weary 2nd Marines had seen their last infantry action on Guadalcanal. A new unit now came into being. It was a composite Marine/Army division, or CAM division, formed from units of the 2nd Marine Divisions and the Americal Division. The directing staff was from the 2nd Division since the entire Americal Division was responsible for the main perimeter.

Two of their regiments, 147th, and 182nd Infantry, moved up to attack in line with the 6th Marines still strung out along the coast. The 8th Marines were pinched out of the front lines by a narrowing attack corridor as inland mountains and hills pressed closer to the coastal trail. The 25th Division advance across this rugged terrain was tasked with outflanking the enemy in the vicinity of Kokumbona, while the CAM Division continued to drive west. On the 23rd, as the CAM troops approached Kokumbona, the infantry of the 1st Battalion surged north from the hills and overran the village and Japanese base. They offered a steady but slight resistance to the American advance and withdrew west toward Cape Esperance.

The Imperial Japanese would not attempt to retake Guadalcanal. These were the orders sent in the Emperor's name. Senior staff officers were dispatched to make sure they were followed. The Imperial Japanese Navy would make its final runs of the Tokyo Express, only this time in reverse, to evacuate the garrison to fight later battles to hold the Solomons. Enemy ships were massing to the northwest. General Patch took steps to guard against overextending his forces. Especially faced with what appeared to be another enemy attempt at reinforcement. He pulled back the 25th Division to bolster the primary perimeter defenses and ordered the CAM Division to continue its attack. Marines and soldiers moved out on January 26, gaining over one thousand yards on the first day and two thousand the next. The Japanese contested every attack—but not in strength.

By January 30, the sole frontline unit in the American advance was the 147th Infantry; the 6th Marines held positions to its rear.

The Japanese destroyer transports made their first run to the island on the night of February 2, evacuating twenty-three hundred men from positions near Cape Esperance. On the night of February 5, they returned and evacuated most *Sendai* survivors, and General Hyakutake and his 7th Army staff.

On February 8, the final evacuation was carried out, and a three thousand man rearguard action was embarked. The Japanese withdrew over eleven thousand men in those three nights and evacuated over thirteen thousand soldiers from Guadalcanal. The Americans would meet many of these soldiers again in later battles, but not the six hundred evacuees who died—too sick and worn out to survive the rescue.

On February 9, American soldiers advancing west and east met at Tenaro village on Cape Esperance. The only Marine ground unit still in action was the 3/10 Marines, supporting the advance. General Patch reported the complete and total defeat of Japanese forces on Guadalcanal. No organized Japanese units remained.

On January 31, the 2nd Marines boarded ships to leave Guadalcanal. As with the 1st Marine Division, some of these men were so beaten down by malaria that they had to be carried on board. Observers were struck again as these young men had considerably aged in the last few months, "with their skin cracked, and furrowed, and wrinkled." On February 9, the rest of the 8th Marines boarded the transports. The 6th Marines, with only six weeks on the island, left on the 19th. All troops headed for Wellington, New Zealand. They left behind, on the island as a legacy of the 2nd Marine Division, 263 men dead.

The total cost of the Guadalcanal campaign to the American ground combat forces was 1,598 officers and men killed. 1,152 of them were Marines.

The wounded totaled 4,709. Of these 2,799 were Marines. Marine aviation casualties were 147 killed and 127 wounded.

The Japanese lost nearly 25,000 on Guadalcanal. About half killed in action—the rest died from wounds, starvation, and illness.

At sea, each side lost a similar number of fighting ships. The Japanese lost two battleships, three carriers, twelve cruisers, and twenty-five destroyers—all were irreplaceable. While the Allied ship losses were substantial and costly: they were not fatal. All lost ships were ultimately replaced. Over six hundred Japanese planes were shot down. Worse than the loss of aircraft was the death of over two thousand experienced pilots and aircrew. The Allied plane losses were only half that of the enemy's number, and the pilot and aircrew losses were substantially lower.

Pres. Roosevelt, awarded Gen. Vandegrift the Medal of Honor for outstanding and heroic accomplishment for his leadership of the American forces on Guadalcanal from August 7 to December 9, 1942. He also awarded a presidential unit citation to the 1st Marine Division for "outstanding gallantry, reflecting courage and determination of an inspiring order."

Included in the division citation and award, besides the organic units of the 1st Division with the 2nd and 8th Marines and attached units of the 2nd Marine Division, all of the Americal Division, the 1st Parachute Battalion, 1st and 2nd Raider Battalions, elements of the 3rd, 5th and, 14th Defense Battalions, the 1st Aviation Engineer Battalion, the 6th Naval Construction Battalion, and two motor torpedo boat squadrons. The vital Cactus Air Force was included. Represented by seven Marine headquarters and service squadrons, sixteen Marine flying squadrons, sixteen Naval flying squadrons, and five Army flying squadrons.

The Guadalcanal victory was a crucial turning point in the Pacific War. The Japanese offensive was ended. The Imperial Japanese pilots, seamen, and infantry had been in close combat with the Americans and their allies. There were still years of fierce fighting ahead, but now there was no question of the eventual outcome.

GENERAL ALEXANDER A. VANDEGRIFT

IF MILITARY TITLES were awarded in America as they were in England, the commanding General of the Marine Corps forces at Guadalcanal would be known as "Vandegrift of Guadalcanal." But America does not give aristocratic titles, nor would such a formality be in keeping with the soft-spoken, modest demeanor of Alexander Vandegrift.

The man who led the 1st Marine Division and America's first ground offensive operation of World War II was born in Charlottesville, Virginia, 1887. His grandfather told him fascinating stories of life in the Confederate Army during the Civil War. It was destiny that young Alexander would settle on a military career. He was commissioned as a Marine lieutenant in 1909. He received an early baptism of fire in 1912 during the bombardment, assault, and capture of Coyotepe in Nicaragua. Two years later, he would take part in the capture and occupation of Veracruz, Mexico. Vandegrift would spend the greater part of his next decade in Haiti. He fought bandits and served as an inspector of constabulary with the *Gendarmerie d'Haiti*. In Haiti, he met and befriended Marine Col. Smedley Butler, who called him "Sunny Jim." The lessons of these years fighting an elusive enemy in a hostile jungle environment were not lost on this young Marine officer.

He spent the next eighteen years in several posts and stations in the United States and two tours of China duty in Tientsin and Peiping. Before Pearl Harbor, Vandegrift was appointed assistant to the Maj. Gen. Commandant, and in 1940 received a single star of a Brig. General. He was dispatched to the 1st Marine Division in November 1941. In May 1942, he sailed for the South Pacific as the commanding general of the 1st Marine Division ever to leave the United States. On August 7, 1942, he told his Marines that "God favors the bold and strong of heart." He led the 1st Marine Division ashore in the

Solomon Islands in the first large-scale offensive against the Japanese.

His victory at Guadalcanal earned him the Medal of Honor, and the Navy Cross, along with the praise of a grateful nation. In July 1943, he took command of I Marine Amphibious Corps. He planned the landings at Empress Agusta Bay, Bougainville, and the Northern Solomons. On November 1, 1943, he was recalled to Washington to be the 18th Commandant of the Marine Corps.

January 1, 1944, as a Lieut. General, he was sworn in as Commandant. On April 4, 1945, he was promoted to General and became the first officer on active duty to attain a four-star rank. In the final stages of the war, Gen. Vandegrift directed an elite force approaching half a million men and women, with its own aviation force. When he compared his Marines to the Japanese, he noted that the Japanese soldier is:

trained to go to a place, stay there, fight, and die. We train our men to go to a place, fight to win, and to live. I assure you, it is a better theory.

Gen. Vandegrift fought another battle in the halls of Congress. The stakes were the survival of the US Marine Corps. His counter testimony during congressional hearings of the spring of 1946 helped to defeat initial attempts to merge or unify the US Armed Forces. Although his term as Commandant ended on December 31, 1947, Gen. Vandegrift lived to see the passage of Public Law 416, which preserved the Corps and its historic mission. He retired on April 1, 1949, after 40 years of service.

Gen. Vandegrift outlived both his wife and their only son. He spent his last years in Delray, Florida. He died on May 8, 1973, at 86 years old.

THE COASTWATCHERS

A GROUP of less than fifteen-hundred native coastwatchers served as the eyes and ears of Allied forces, reporting Japanese movements and units on the ground, in the air, and at sea. The coastwatchers, code named Ferdinand, possessed both physical and mental courage having to perform their jobs in remote jungle outposts. Their invaluable knowledge of the geography and peoples of the Pacific made them an indispensable addition to the Allied war effort.

This concept originated in 1919 by a proposal from the Royal Australian Navy to form a civilian coast watching organization for an early warning in case of invasion. When war broke out in 1939, over eight hundred people served as coastwatchers. They manned observation posts mainly on the Australian coast. They were government officials aided by missionaries and planters who, with the war growing closer with Japan, were placed under the intelligence and control of the Australian Navy. By 1942, the coast watching system and the accompanying intelligence network covered an area of over half-a-million miles. They were now placed under the control of the Allied Intelligence Bureau (AIB). The AIB coordinate needed all Allied intelligence activities in the Southwest Pacific. Their initial principal mission was to collect all information about the enemy near Guadalcanal.

Coastwatchers were useful to Marine forces in providing reports on the number and movement of the Japanese troops. 1st Division Marine officers obtained accurate location information of enemy forces and their objective areas. They were provided vital reports on approaching Japanese bombing raids. On August 8, 1942, coastwatcher Jack Reed, on Bougainville, alerted American forces to an upcoming raid by over forty Japanese bombers. This resulted in thirty-six enemy planes shot down and destroyed. The coastwatchers provided an early warning system that helped the Marine forces on Guadalcanal maintain control of the Henderson Field airstrip.

The coastwatchers also rescued over 115 Allied pilots, including Marines, during the Solomon Islands campaign. Often frequently in danger or at a risk to their own lives. The pipe-smoking coastwatcher Jack Reed coordinated the evacuation on Bougainville of four nuns and twenty-five civilians with the US submarine *Nautilus*.

It's unknown the exact number of coastwatchers that paid the ultimate price in the performance of their duties. Many brave men and women died in anonymity, without knowing the contribution their services had made to the ultimate victory in the Pacific Theatre. Perhaps they'd be gratified to know that no less an authority than Adm. "Bull" Halsey recorded that the coastwatchers saved Guadalcanal—and Guadalcanal saved the Pacific.

SERGEANT MAJOR SIR JACOB CHARLES VOUZA

BORN IN 1900 AT TASIMBOKO, Guadalcanal, and the British Solomon Islands protectorate. He was educated at the South

Seas evangelical mission school. He joined the Solomon Islands protectorate Armed Constabulary In 1916. In 1941 he retired at the rank of sergeant major after twenty-five-years of service.

After the Imperial Japanese invaded his home island, he volunteered to work with the coastwatchers on active duty with the British forces. Vouza's experience as a scout had already been established when the 1st Marine Division landed on Guadalcanal. On August 7, 1942, he rescued a down naval pilot from the *USS Wasp*, who was shot down inside Japanese territory. He guided the pilot to friendly lines where he met the Marines for the first time.

Vouza volunteered to scout behind enemy lines for the Marines. On August 27, he was captured by the Japanese while on a Marine Corps mission to locate suspected enemy lookouts. The Japanese found a small American flag in his loincloth. He was tied to a tree and interrogated about Allied forces. Vouza was questioned for hours, but refused to talk. He was tortured. Bayoneted in the arms, stomach, throat, face, and left to die.

After his captors departed, he freed himself. He made his way through miles of jungle to the American lines. He supplied valuable intelligence information to the Marines about an impending Japanese attack before accepting medical attention. He spent twelve days in the hospital, then returned to duty as chief scout for the Marines. He accompanied. Col. Carlson in the 2nd Marine Raider Battalion when they made their thirty-day raid behind enemy lines at Guadalcanal.

Sgt. Maj. Vouza was highly decorated for his World War II service. The Silver Star was presented to him personally by Gen. Vandegrift for refusing to give information under Japanese torture. He was also awarded the Legion of Merit for outstanding service with the 2nd Raider Battalion during November and December 1942.

After the war, Sgt. Major Vouza continued to serve his fellow islanders. In 1949 he was appointed district headman and president of the Guadalcanal Council. From 1952 to 1958, he was a member of the British Solomon Islands Protectorate Advisory Council.

During his long association with the US Marine Corps and through the years, he made many friends. In 1968, he visited the United States and was the honored guest of the 1st Marine Division Association. In 1979 he was knighted by Britain's Queen Elizabeth II. He died on March 15, 1984.

THE AMTRAC LVT 1 (LANDING VEHICLE, TRACKED, MARK 1)

THE MARINE CORPS was developing an amphibious warfare doctrine during the 1920s and 30s. There was a need for a motorized amphibian vehicle to transport men and equipment from ships across reefs and beaches into battle. Especially when the beach was defended.

The Marines adopted the LVT 1 in 1940. Designed by Donald Roebling and known as the "Amtrac" (amphibian tractor), The LVT 1 had a front cabin and a small engine compartment in the rear. The bulk of the body was used as a carrying space. During the next three years, over twelve hundred amphibious tractors were built and used in the war. The Amtrac was constructed of welded steel and propelled on both land and water by paddle-type treads. It functioned as a supply vehicle. It could carry forty-five-hundred-pounds of cargo. In August 1942, the Amtrac saw combat on Guadal-canal with the 1st Amphibian Tractor Battalion. Fighting throughout the Solomon Islands campaigns, the Amtrac provided Marines of all types logistical support, moving thou-sands-of-tons of supplies from the front lines. They were also pressed into a more tactical use. They moved artillery pieces, they held defensive positions, and occasionally supported Marines in the attack with their machine guns. They were also used as pontoons to support bridges across Guadalcanal rivers.

The Amtrac proved to be more seaworthy than a boat of comparable size. They remained afloat with its entire cargo hold full of water, but defects in the design soon became apparent. The paddle treads on the tracks and the rigid suspension system were both susceptible to damage when driven on land. They did not provide the desired speed on land or water. The Amtrac performed well when used against undefended beachheads, but the lack of armor made it an easy target for enemy attacks against the heavily defended Pacific Islands. This was an obvious weakness during the fighting in the Solomon Islands, but Amtracs with improvised armor were still in use at the assault on Tarawa, where over 75% of them were lost in three days.

The Amtrac proved its value and validated the amphibious vehicle concept through the excellent mobility and versatility it demonstrated throughout many campaigns in the Pacific. Although designed solely for supply purposes, it was first thrust into combat use in early war engagements. Its initial role as a support vehicle to deliver ammunition, supplies, and reinforcements made the difference between victory and defeat.

REISING GUN

Eugene Reising designed and developed this extraordinary gun. The Reising gun was patented in 1940 and manufactured by the gun-making firm of Harrington and Richardson in Worcester, Massachusetts. According to research, the guns were made on existing machine tools that dated back to the Civil War, and of ordinary steel rather than steel ordinance.

New machine tools and ordinance steel were scarce and needed for more demanding weapons. This meant the Reising gun met an immediate requirement for many submachine guns at the time. When the production of the Thompson M1928 and M1 submachine guns hadn't yet caught up with the demand, the stamped out M3 "grease gun" had still not yet been invented.

The Reising gun came in two different models, the 50 and the 55. The model 50 had a wooden stock and a compensator attached to the muzzle. The compensator, which reduced the upward muzzle climb from the recoil, was invented by Richard Cutts and his son; both were to become Marine brigadier generals.

The other version was dubbed the model 55. It had a folding metal wire shoulder stock which swiveled on a wooden pistol grip. It also had a shorter barrel and no compensator. Intended for use by the parachutists, tank crews, and others needing a compact weapon. Both versions of the Reising gun fired .45-caliber ammunition, the same cartridge as the automatic Colt pistol and the Thompson machine gun. Over one hundred thousand Reising submachine guns were produced between 1940 and 1942.

Some small numbers of these weapons were acquired by Great Britain and the Soviet Union. Most were used by the Marine Corps in the Solomon Islands campaign. The model 55 was issued to both the Marine Parachute Battalion and Raiders fighting on Guadalcanal. After its lackluster performance in combat, it was withdrawn from frontline service in 1943 due to many flaws in design and manufacture.

The Reising's major flaws were the propensity for jamming. This was because of a design problem in the magazine, and the fact that the magazines were made of a soft sheet steel. The weapon safety mechanism didn't always work. If the butt was slammed down on the deck, the hammer would set back against the mainspring and then fly forward, firing a chambered cartridge. This design allowed the entry of dirt into the mechanism, and close tolerances caused it to jam. The steel used allowed excessive rust to form in the tropical humidity of the Solomons. At six pounds, the Reising was handier than the ten pound Thompson, more accurate, easier to shoot, and more reliable under other than combat conditions, but the muzzle always needed to be pointed in a safe direction. The model 50 was also issued to Marines for guard duty at posts and stations in the United States.

THE JAPANESE 50MM HEAVY GRENADE DISCHARGER

KNOWN as the *Juteki* by the Japanese, this weapon was designated as "heavy," being justified by the powerful one pound, 12-ounce high explosive shell it fired. It also fired the standard model 91 fragmentation grenade.

The American Marines and soldiers who first encountered this weapon and others of its kind in combat named them "knee mortars," because they were fired from a kneeling position. The dischargers concave baseplate was firmly pressed into the surface of the ground by the operator's foot to support the heavy recoil of the fired shell.

The term knee mortars suggested to some untrained captors of these weapons that they were to be fired with the baseplate resting against the knee or thigh. When a Marine fired one of these from his thigh and broke his upper leg bone, efforts were swiftly undertaken in the field to immediately educate all combat troops in the safe and proper handling of these useful weapons.

The 50mm heavy grenade discharger is a muzzle-loaded, high-angle fire weapon that weighs ten pounds and is twenty-four inches in overall length. Its design is compact and straightforward. The discharger has three major components: the supporting barrel pedestal with a firing mechanism, the baseplate, and the rifled barrel. Operation of this model was straightforward, and with practice, the user could deliver accurate fire quickly to a target.

In all significant battles of the Pacific, the 50mm heavy grenade discharger was an uncomplicated, portable, and efficient weapon. Transported in a leather case wrapped in a cloth with a sling. Its one-piece construction made it easy to bring into action rapidly. This grenade discharger had the advantage over most mortars. It could be aimed and fired mechanically after the projectile had been placed in the barrel.

The model 91 fragmentation grenade with its seven-second fuse made this discharger effective in a jungle setting. Offering the user complete safety from a premature detonation by the overhanging foliage. It fired an incendiary grenade and signal and smoke shells, which made this versatile and effective weapon valuable with its particular types of ammunition.

This weapon won the respect of all those who came to know it.

1ST MARINE UTILITY UNIFORM ISSUED IN WORLD WAR II

When the United States Marine Corps entered World War II, they wore the same summer field uniform they had worn during the Banana Wars. The Marines that defended American Pacific outposts on Guam, Philippines, and Wake Island in the late months of 1941 wore a summer field uniform that consisted of a khaki cotton shirt and trousers, leggings, and a steel helmet. Plans to change this uniform had been underway for over a year before the opening of hostilities.

Just like the Army, the Marine Corps had used a loose-fitting blue denim fatigue uniform for details and field exercises since the 1920s. This fatigue uniform came in either a two-piece bib overalls and jacket or a one-piece coverall with USMC metal buttons. It was ultimately replaced in June 1940 by a green cotton coverall. This uniform and the same summer field uniform were replaced by what would become known as the utility uniform. Approved for use on the 166th birthday of the Marine Corps, November 10, 1941. This uniform was made of a sage green (also known as olive drab) herringbone twill cotton, at the time a popular material for civilian work clothing. The two-piece uniform consisted of a coat (referred to as a jacket by Marines) and trousers. In 1943, a cap of the same material would be issued.

The loose-fitting coat was closed down the front by 24 riveted, bronze finish, steel buttons; each bore the words "USMC" in relief. The cuffs were closed by similar buttons. Two large patch pockets were sewn on the front skirts of the jacket and a single patch pocket was stitched to the left breast. The pocket had the Marine Corps eagle, globe, anchor, and an insignia with USMC letters stenciled on it in black ink. The trousers could be worn with or without khaki canvas leggings and had two rear patch pockets and two front pockets.

This new uniform was issued to the flood of new recruits that crowded depots in the early months of 1942. First worn in combat during the landing on Guadalcanal in August 1942, this uniform was worn by Marines of all arms from the Solomon campaigns until the end of the war. Initially, the buttons on the coat and the trousers were all copper plated. An emergency alternate specification was approved on August 15, 1942, eight days after the landing on Guadalcanal. This allowed for a variety of finishes on the buttons. Toward the end of the war, a new "modified" utility uniform had been developed after Tarawa was issued. Besides a variety of camouflage uniforms, these utility uniforms, along with Army designed M1 helmets. The Marine Corps wore rubber-soled "boondocker" shoes that would be worn throughout the war in the Pacific, during the postwar years, and into the Korean War.

THE 1ST MARINE DIVISION PATCH

THE 1ST DIVISION shoulder patch was authorized to be worn by members of units attached or organic to the division and its four landings in the Pacific War. It was the 1st unit patch to be allowed for wear in World War II. Specifically, it commemorated the division's sacrifices and victory in the invasion and battle for Guadalcanal.

Before the 1st Division left Guadalcanal for Australia, there was a discussion by senior staff about uniforms and the troops. At first, the Marines would have to wear US Army uniforms. Which meant they'd lose their identity and so the idea came up for a division patch. After several different designs were proposed, General Vandegrift ultimately approved one on the flight out of Guadalcanal.

Capt. Donald Dixon drew a diamond in his notebook, and in the middle of the diamond, he doodled the numeral one. He sketched the word Guadalcanal down its length. He believed the entire operation had been under the southern cross, so he drew that in as well. An hour later, he took his drawing to the front of the aircraft to Gen. Vandegrift. The general enthusiastically approved his design and wrote his initials on the bottom of the notebook page.

After Capt. Dixon arrived in Brisbane, Australia. He bought a child's watercolor set while confined to his hotel room because of malaria. He drew a bunch of diamonds on a big sheet, he colored each one differently. He then took samples to Gen. Vandegrift, who chose the one colored a shade of blue that he liked. Then Dixon took the sketch to the Australian knitting mills to have it produced. He offered the credit of the posting exchange funds to pay for manufacturing the patches. After a week, the patches rolled off the knitting machines, and Capt. Dixon was there to approve them. He recalled:

After they came off the machine, I picked up a sheet of them. They looked excellent, and when they were cut, I picked up one of the Patches. It was the first off the knitting machine.

The division's post exchanges sold the patches almost immediately. The Marines bought extras to give away as souvenirs to their Australian friends or send home.

Newly established Marine divisions, as well as the raider battalions, parachute battalions, the aircraft wings, seagoing Marines, fleet Marine force Pacific units, and others, were all now allowed to have their own distinctive patch, a total of thirty-three, following the lead of the 1st Marine Division. The Marines that returned to the United States for duty or leave were authorized to wear the insignia until assigned to another unit. Many 1st Division men joining another unit and having to relinquish the wearing of their 1st Division patch were annoyed. After the war, Capt. Dixon went to Gen. Vandegrift and told him he no longer believed Marines should wear anything on their uniforms to distinguish them from other Marines. Vandegrift agreed, and the patches came off for good.

THE GEORGE MEDAL

THE GEORGE METAL was legendary among 1st Marine Division veterans of Guadalcanal. Only fifty were cast in Australia before the mold broke. This medal commemorated the difficult divisional switch during the early Guadalcanal days. Back when food, ammunition, and heavy equipment were in short supply, and the Japanese had plenty. When the issue was no longer in doubt, the Marines reflected on the D-Day plus three Navy withdrawals in the face of increasing Japanese air attacks and surface action, leaving the divisions in a tight spot.

Capt. Donald Dixon again resolved to commemorate the occasion. He designed an appropriate medal using a fifty-cent piece to draw a circle on the captured Japanese blank military postcard. Capt. Dixon's design was approved, and when the division got to Australia, the mold was made by a local craftsman. Only a small number were capped before the mold became unserviceable. The Marines that wanted a medal, paid one Australian pound and received a certificate. These medals are now an even greater rarity than at the time.

The medal design shows a hand and sleeve dropping a hot potato shaped like Guadalcanal into the arms of a Marine. The original design for the sleeve stripes were from Admiral Gormley or Admiral Fletcher, but the final medal diplomatically omitted the style of identification.

On the opposite side is a cactus, indigenous to Arizona, not Guadalcanal, but representing the codename for the island, "Cactus." The inscription is *Facia Georgius*, "Let George do it." This is how it became known as the George Medal. On the medal's reverse shows a picture of a cow (the original design was a Japanese soldier with his breaches down) and electric fan, and is inscribed: "in fond remembrance of the happy days spent from August 7, 1942, to January 5, 1943, USMC." The suspension ribbon was made from the pale green herringbone twill from a Marines utility uniform. The legend has it that for it to be authentic, the utilities from which the ribbons were made had to have been washed in the waters of Guadalcanal's Lunga River.

OPERATION GALVANIC

1943 BATTLE FOR TARAWA

INTRODUCTION

In August 1943, Admiral Spruance, the Central Pacific Naval Force Commander, met in secret with Gen. Julian Smith and other 2nd Marine Division staff officers. Adm. Spruance told the Marines to prepare for an amphibious assault in the

Gilbert Islands by November. The Marines were well aware of the Gilbert Islands. Under Colonel Evans Carlson, the 2nd Marine Raider Battalion had attacked Makin only a year before. Intelligence reported that the Japanese had fortified Betio Island in the Tarawa Atoll. Imperial Japanese Marines guarded an airstrip that Adm. Spruance designated the prime target for the 2nd Marines.

Colonel Shoup was Gen. Smith's operation officer. He studied Betio's primitive chart and saw the tiny island was surrounded by a barrier reef. Col. Shoup asked if any of the Navy's shallow draft experimental plastic boats would be provided. He was disappointed to hear that only the usual wooden landing craft would be available for this assault. The operation on Tarawa had become a tactical watershed. This would be the first large-scale test of American amphibious forces against a strongly fortified beachhead. The Marine assault on Tarawa Atoll's islet, Betio, was one of World War II Pacific Theater's bloodiest. After the assault, *Time* magazine published its post-battle analysis:

Over three thousand United States Marines, mostly now dead or wounded, gave the nation a new name to stand behind those of Concord Bridge, the Bon Homme Richard, Little Big Horn, the Alamo, and Belleau Wood. This new name is Tarawa.

THE YOGAKI PLAN

G E I C
TARAWA ATOLL
TRACED FROM DOS TRIANGULATION SURVEY

THE GILBERT ISLANDS comprise sixteen scattered atolls along the equator in the Central Pacific. Tarawa Atoll is over 2,000 miles southwest of Pearl Harbor and 540 miles southeast of the Marshall Islands. Betio is the principal islet in the Tarawa Atoll.

Three days after Pearl Harbor, the Japanese seized Makin and Tarawa from the British. After a raid in August 1942, the Japanese realized their vulnerability in the Gilbert Island chain. After the attack, the *6th Yokosuka Special Naval Landing Force* was dispatched to the islands, led by Admiral Saichiro, a well-known engineer. He directed the construction of advanced and sophisticated defensive positions on the Tarawa Atoll. Adm. Saichiro's vision was to make Tarawa so formidable that any American amphibious assault would stall at the water's edge, and allow the Japanese time to annihilate the landing force.

The Japanese strategy was outlined in the *Yogaki* Plan. Its principal point was to defend Eastern Micronesia from an Allied invasion. Admiral Nimitz took the Japanese threat of counterattack with bombers, submarines, and their main battle fleet, seriously. Adm. Nimitz told Spruance, "Get the hell in and the hell out." The overall theme of this island assault was to seize the Gilbert Island targets with lightning speed.

Codename "Operation Galvanic" was assigned by the Joint Chiefs of Staff to capture Tarawa and Makin in the Gilbert Islands. The 2nd Marine Division was given the invasion of Tarawa while the Army's 165th Regimental Combat Team would assault Makin. All three of the landing force commanders assigned to Operation Galvanic had the last name Smith. The senior general was Holland "Howling Mad" Smith, who commanded the V Amphibious Corps. General Julian Smith commanded the 2nd Marines. And General Ralph Smith was in charge of the 27th Infantry Division.

Admiral Kelly Turner, a veteran of the bloody Guadalcanal Campaign, was assigned command of all amphibious assault forces for Operation Galvanic. Adm. Turner was accompanied by Gen. Holland Smith and was given Task Force 52 for the assault on Makin.

Admiral Harry Hill was assigned command of Task Force 53 for the assault on Tarawa. Gen. Julian Smith and Adm. Harry Hill discussed the plans on board the battleship *Maryland*. These two officers couldn't be more different. Adm. Hill was impetuous and outspoken, while Gen. Smith was reflective and reserved. They worked together well and outlined a plan for the assault on the Gilbert Islands. Adm. Spruance set the D-Day for November 20, 1943.

Col. Shoup came up with an outline for tackling Betio's barrier reefs. The Marines used LVT-1s (Landing Vehicle Tracked or "Alligators"), an amphibian tractor, during Guadalcanal. The Alligators were unarmored logistical vehicles. They were not assault craft, but true amphibians— capable of being launched at sea and moving through moderate surf to reach the shore. Col. Shoup discussed the potential idea of using the LVT assault craft with the 2nd Amphibian Tractor Battalion commander, Major Henry Drews. The major liked the idea but warned Shoup that many tractors were in poor condition after the Guadalcanal Campaign. Maj. Drews could provide only seventy-five Alligators—nowhere near enough to transport all the assault waves. Worse, the thin hulled tractors were vulnerable to enemy fire and would need armor plating. Col. Shoup ordered Maj. Drews to modify the tractors with whatever armor plating he could scrounge together.

Gen. Julian Smith knew that the armored LVT-2s, known as "Water Buffalo", were stockpiled in San Diego. He submitted an urgent request for one hundred newer models to be dispatched immediately. Gen. Holland Smith endorsed the request while Adm. Turner disagreed. The argument was intense. Adm. Turner did not dispute the need for Marines to have a reef crossing capability. He objected to the fact these newly ordered vehicles would need to be transported to Tarawa. They'd require LSTs (Tank Landing Ships). The LSTs slow speed (8 knots max) would require an additional convoy, independent escorts, and increased risk of losing the initiative and strategic surprise. Gen. Smith reduced the debate to the essentials:

No LVTs, No operation.

Adm. Turner eventually agreed, but it would not be a complete victory for the 2nd Marines. Fifty of the new one hundred LVT-2s would support the Army's landing at Makin against a lighter opposition. The Marine vehicles scheduled to arrive would not be there in time for any workup training or rehearsal landings. The first time the Marine Infantry would lay eyes on the LVT-2s would be in the predawn hours of Tarawa's D-Day—if at all.

TASK FORCE 53

REPLACEMENT TROOPS POURED into New Zealand. Gen. Smith requested the reassignment of Colonel Edson to be his division chief of staff. The fiery Col. Edson was now a Marine Corps legend for his heroic exploits on Guadalcanal. He worked tirelessly to forge the new recruits and veterans into an effective amphibious assault team. The intelligence reports from Betio were startling. The island was void of any natural fortifications to conceal enemy fire. And too narrow, inhibiting any maneuvering room, which favored the Japanese. Betio was 800 yards at its widest point and less than three miles long. It also contained no natural elevation higher than ten feet above sea level. Col. Edson observed that every place on the island could be covered by machine gun and direct rifle fire.

These elaborate defenses were prepared by Adm. Saichiro. He used minefields, long strings of barbed wire to protect beach approaches, and concrete and steel pillboxes and bunkers. The Japanese built a barrier of coral and logs around much of the islands. They use tank traps to protect fortified command bunkers and firing positions inland of the beach. Of the island's five hundred pillboxes, most were covered by steel plates, logs, and sand.

The Japanese defenders on the island had 8-inch turret-mounted naval rifles, "Singapore guns." They also had many anti-aircraft, anti-boat, heavy caliber coastal defense and field artillery guns, and howitzers. They had an abundant amount of 50mm mortars, dual-purpose 13mm heavy machine guns, and light tanks with 37mm guns. During August, the Japanese high command replaced Saichiro with Admiral Shibasaki, an officer with a reputation for being more of a fighter than an engineer.

Intelligence estimated the total strength of the enemy garrison on Betio was 4,800 men. Twenty-six hundred of them were Imperial Japanese Marines, first-rate naval troops, nicknamed "Tojo's best." Col. Edson's 1st Raider Battalion had taken nearly 100 casualties wrestling Tulagi from these elite Japanese naval troops in the previous August. Adm. Shibasaki boasted that a million Americans couldn't take Tarawa in a hundred years. His optimism was understandable at the time, because Tarawa was the most heavily defended island ever invaded by Allied forces in the Pacific.

Task Force 53 desperately needed detailed tide information. Col. Shoup was confident that the LVTs could negotiate the reef during any tide. Still, the rest of the tanks, artillery, assault troops, and reserve forces would need to come ashore in Higgins boats (LCVPs). The water depth over the reef was four feet, it was enough to float a loaded Higgins boat. If less than four feet, the troops would need to wade several hundred yards ashore against an array of deadly Japanese weapons.

A New Zealand reserve officer, with fifteen years' experience sailing Tarawa's waters, predicted: "there won't even be 3 feet of water on that reef when the assault begins."

Col. Shoup took his warning seriously and made sure that all troops knew in advance that there would be a 50-50 chance of having to wade ashore. Besides the island's physical constraints and daunting Japanese defenses, Col. Shoup proposed a landing plan that included a preliminary bombardment and advance seizure of neighboring Bairiki Islands, to be used as an artillery firebase and a decoy landing. Gen. Smith took this proposal to Pearl Harbor and recommended it to the significant officers involved in Operation Galvanic: Admirals Spruance, Turner and Nimitz, and Gen. Holland Smith.

The restrictions imposed by CinCPac were sobering. Adm. Nimitz declared that the requirement for strategic surprise would limit any bombardment of Betio to only three hours on the morning of D-Day. He also ruled out Bairiki's advance seizure and any decoy landings to defend against the Japanese fleet. To make things worse, Gen. Holland Smith announced that the 6th Marines would be withheld and used as a reserve force. The 2nd Marine Division's tactical options had been stripped away. Ordered into a frontal assault against the teeth of Japanese defenses on Betio with only a three-hour bombardment. Without the 6th Marines attacking the island fortress, that would mean only a 2:1 troop superiority—well below the doctrinal minimum.

Col. Shoup returned to New Zealand and prepared a modified operations order and selected the landing beaches. The southwestern tip of Tarawa near the lagoon entrance looked like the profile of a crested bird lying on its back. The Japanese concentrated their defenses on the southern and western coasts (the bird's head and back). Northern beaches had calmer lagoon waters and only one deadly exception. Defenses in this sector were incomplete, but being improved daily. A thousand-yard pier that jutted north over the fringing reef into deeper lagoon waters (the bird's legs, sticking upward) was an attractive logistics target. He selected the northern coast for landing beaches—but there was no safe avenue of approach.

The northern shore of Betio from the departure line

within the lagoon was designated for the three landing beaches, each 600 yards in length. Moving from west to east, Red Beach One, made up the bird's beak and neck from the northwestern tip of Betio to a point just east, Red Beach Two made up the bird's breast from the juncture to the pier, and Red Beach Three from the pier eastward. Green Beach on the western shore, along with other beaches, would be designated as contingencies.

Gen. Smith planned to land with two regiments abreast and one in reserve. Losing the 6th Marines forced him to make a significant change. Col. Shoup's modified plan now assigned the 2nd Marines, reinforced by 2/8 (2nd Battalion, 8th Marines) as the main assault force. The rest of the 8th Marines would make up the divisional reserve. An advanced seizure of the pier by First Lieutenant Hawkin's Scout-Sniper Platoon would precede the main assault.

Gen. Smith scheduled a large-scale amphibious exercise in Hawkes Bay on November 1. He planned for New Zealand trucks to haul the men back to Wellington at the end for a large dance. The entire 2nd Marine Division boarded the sixteen amphibious ships for the routine exercise. It was all a ruse. The ships weighed anchor and headed north to begin Operation Galvanic.

Task Force 53 assembled in New Hebrides on November 7. Adm. Hill arrived onboard the *Maryland*. Now that the Marines were keenly aware and operations were underway, they were more interested in the fourteen new Sherman tanks on board the *Ashland*. The 2nd Marine Division had never operated with medium tanks before. The rehearsal landings did little to prepare the Marines for the assault on Betio. Fleet carriers and air wings were assaulting other targets in the Solomons. Sherman tanks had nowhere to offload: the new LVT-2s were still somewhere to the north, underway for Tarawa. And naval gunships were bombarding Erradaka Island, away from the troops landing at Mele Bay.

One positive aspect of the amphibious assault rehearsal was that the Marines could practice embarking on rubber rafts. In the prewar Fleet Marine Force, the first battalion in each regiment was designated the Rubber Boat Battalion. This common site of a mini-flotilla inspired catcalls from other Marines. The main contentious issue during the post-rehearsal critique was the naval gunfire plan. The target island would receive the greatest concentration of naval gunfire in the war to date. Adm. Turner was optimistic about the outcome; he made his plans clear that they did not intend to just neutralize or destroy the island—but obliterate it. Gen. Smith reminded the senior naval officers that the Marines crossed the beach with bayonets. Their only armor would be khaki shirts.

While on New Hebrides, Colonel Marshall, the commander of Combat Team Two became too ill to continue. Gen. Smith promoted Col. Shoup to relieve Col. Marshall. Shoup knew the 2nd Marines, and he knew the plan. The architect was now the executor.

Once underway, Adm. Hill ordered the various commanders of Task Force 53 to brief troops on the destination and mission. Tarawa was a surprise to most of the men. Many had believed they were heading for Wake Island. On the day before D-Day, Gen. Smith sent a message to the 2nd Division officers and men. In his message, he reassured his men that the Navy would stay and provide support throughout the campaign—unlike in the Guadalcanal Campaign. The troops attentively listened to these words coming over the loud-speakers:

We are embarked on a great offensive to destroy the enemy in the Central Pacific. The Navy will screen our operation and support our attack tomorrow with the greatest concentration of naval gunfire and aerial bombardment in the history of war. The Navy will remain with us until our objective has been secured. Garrison troops are already en route to relieve us as soon as we have completed our work. Good luck and God bless you all.

As the sun set on Task Force 53 on the evening of D -1, it seemed strategic surprise had been attained. More good news came with the report that small convoys of LSTs transporting the LVT-2s arrived safely from Samoa and had joined the formation. All the pieces were coming together.

D-DAY AT BETIO

Shortly after midnight on D-Day, the crowded transports of Task Force 53 arrived off Tarawa. The sailors cheered as the public address system played the Marine Hymn to the 2/2

Marines scrambling over the sides and down the cargo nets at 0320.

This was when things started to go wrong.

Adm. Hill, the amphibious task force commander, realized the transports were in the wrong anchorage. He directed the fire support ships to immediately shift to the correct site. While the landing craft bobbed away along in the wake of the ships, several Marines were halfway down the cargo nets when the ships unexpectedly weighed anchor. Choppy seas made matching the exact LVTs with their assigned assault teams dangerous in the darkness.

Few tactical plans survived the opening rounds of execution in this amphibious operation. The D-Day plan was for the H-Hour assault wave to start at 0830. A fast carrier strike would initiate the action with a thirty-minute bombing raid at 0545. After that, the fire support ships would bombard the island from a close range for the next two hours. The planes would then return for a final strafing run, five minutes before H-Hour, and then shift to inland targets while the Marine Corps stormed ashore.

None of this went according to plan.

The Japanese were alerted by the predawn activities offshore and initiated the battle. Their garrison opened fire on Task Force 53 with big naval guns at 0505. The *Maryland's* and *Colorado's* main batteries returned fire at once, and several 16-inch shells found their mark. A huge fireball signaled the destruction of an enemy ammunition bunker at one of the Japanese's gun positions. After other fire support ships joined in, Adm. Hill ordered a cease-fire thirty-five minutes later. He'd expected the air attack to begin. A long silence and no air assault.

The carrier air group changed plans. They postponed the strike by thirty minutes. Their modifications were never relayed to Adm. Hill. Hill's problems were aggravated by the communication loss on his flagship after the ship's main battery's initial crushing salvo. The Japanese coastal defense guns were damaged, but still dangerous. This mistake gave the Japanese almost thirty minutes to adjust and recover. Adm. Hill was frustrated at every turn and ordered his ships to resume firing at 0605. At 0610, carrier fast attack planes appeared. They bombed and strafed the island for the next few minutes. Throughout this confusion, the sun rose into a macabre background of thick, black smoke.

The destroyers, cruisers, and battleships of Task Force 53 bombarded Betio for the next few hours. The shock and awe of the shelling was a vivid experience for the Marines. A combat photographer, Staff Sergeant Hatch, recalled:

> *We really didn't see how we could do anything but just go in there and bury the Japanese. This wasn't even going to be a fight. Surely no mortal man could live through this destroying power. Any Japs on the island would have to be dead by now.*

SSgt. Hatch was proved wrong by a geyser of water fifty yards to the starboard side of his ship. The Japanese resumed fire and targeted the vulnerable troop transports underway for the second time that morning.

Gen. Smith and Adm. Hill onboard *Maryland* struggled to get information throughout the long day. Their best source of information was from a Kingfisher observation aircraft, launched by the battleships. Adm. Hill asked the pilot if the reef was covered with water and received a negative answer. The first wave of LVTs, with over seven hundred embarked Marines, left the assembly area and headed toward the departure line.

The embarked Marines in the LVTs had a difficult, long morning. Cross deck transfers were dangerous in choppy seas while 8-inch shells exploded around them. They began a long run to the beach—ten miles away. The LVTs started on time but fell behind schedule quickly. The LVT-1s of the first wave failed to maintain the 4-knot speed of advance due to a strong westerly current. This, combined with the weight of the improvised armor plating, reduced the buoyancy. A psychological factor was also at work. Col. Edson had criticized the LVT crews for landing five minutes early during the rehearsal. He had made it clear that early arrival was inexcusable and preferred a late arrival. The three struggling columns of LVTs would not make the beach by the intended hour of 0830. This caused H-Hour to be postponed twice to 0900. All hands did not receive this information.

Two destroyers, *Dashiell* and *Ringgold*, entered the lagoon, following the minesweepers to provide close fire support. Once in the lagoon, the minesweeper *Pursuit* became the primary control ship and directly took a position on the departure line. The *Pursuit* turned her searchlights seaward and provided the LVTs with a beacon of light through the thick smoke and dust. At 0825, as the first wave of LVTs crossed the line, they were still 6,000 yards away from the target beaches.

Minutes after, carrier aircraft roared over Betio, right on time for the original H-Hour but unaware of the new times. Adm. Turner specifically provided all of the players in Operation Galvanic with this warning:

Times to strafe the beaches regarding H-Hour approximate. The distance of the boat from the beach will be a governing factor.

Adm. Hill called them off. The assault planes remained on station with depleted ammunition and fuel levels.

The LVTs chugged shoreward in three long waves. They were separated by 300-yard intervals. Wave One contained forty-two LVT-1s, followed by Wave Two with twenty-four

LVT-2s, and Wave Three with twenty-one LVT-2s. Behind these tracked vehicles were Waves Four and Five of Higgins boats. Each of the assault battalion commanders were in Wave Four. Astern, the *Ashland* ballasted down and launched fourteen LCMs (or Landing Craft Mechanized), all carrying a medium Sherman tank. Four other LCMs trailed, transporting light tanks with 37mm guns.

Just before 0800, Col. Shoup and elements of his tactical command post debarked and headed to the line of departure. A bulky sergeant stood close to Col. Shoup and shielded the radio from the salt spray. Of all the communication failures and blackouts on D-Day, Col. Shoup's radio remained functional longer. It served him better than radios of any other commander—Japanese or American—on the island.

At 0854, Adm. Hill ordered a cease-fire, even though the assault waves were still 4,000 yards out from shore. Col. Edson and Gen. Smith objected. Still, Adm. Hill considered the enormous pillars of smoke unsafe for overhead fire support. After the bombing ceased, the LVTs made their final approach into the teeth of long-range machine-gun fire and artillery airbursts. The artillery could have been fatal to troops crowded into the open-topped LVTs, but the Japanese had loaded the projectiles with high explosives instead of steel shell fragments, which only doused the Marines with "hot sand." This was the last tactical mistake the Japanese made on D-Day.

The aborted airstrike returned at 0855 for five minutes of ineffective strafing along the beaches. The pilots followed their wristwatches instead of the progress of the lead LVTs. Two naval landing boats started toward the end of the long pier at the reef's edge. 1stLt. Hawkins and his Scout Sniper Battalion with a squad of combat engineers charged out. They made quick work of Japanese gun placements along the pier with their flamethrowers and explosives.

The LVTs of Wave One struck the beach and crawled

over the reef. These parts of Col. Shoup's plan were executed flawlessly. The bombardment, as extraordinary as it had been, failed to soften the Japanese defenses. Little of the ships' fire had been directed against the landing beaches.

Adm. Shibasaki vowed to defeat the amphibious assault units at the water's edge. The well-protected Japanese shook off the sand and manned their guns. The curbing of all naval gunfire for the first thirty minutes of the assault was a fateful mistake for Adm. Hill. This gave the Japanese time to shift their forces from the southern and western beaches to reinforce the northern positions. The Japanese defenders were stunned and groggy from the naval pounding and sight of the LVTs crossing the barrier reef. However, Adm. Shibasaki's killing zone was still intact. The Japanese met the amphibious assault waves with a steady volume of combined arms fire.

The first wave of LVTs approaching the final 200 yards of beaches Red One and Red Two were the most challenging. Well aimed fire from anti-boat, 40mm, and heavy and light machine guns hammered the Marines. The assault team fired back with their .50-caliber machine guns mounted on each of the LVT-1s, firing over 10,000 rounds. The exposed gunners were easy targets, and dozens were cut down. The LVT battalion commander, Maj. Drews—who worked with Shoup to make this assault possible—took over a machine gun from a fallen crewman and was killed instantly by a bullet through his eye. One of Maj. Drew's company commanders mentioned later he saw a Japanese officer standing defiantly on the seawall, waving his pistol, "just daring us to come ashore."

The LVTs pushed through. The touchdown times staggered at intervals of ten minutes on each beach. The first LVT to land was a vehicle nicknamed "My Deloris," driven by PFC Moore. My Deloris was the right guide vehicle on Red Beach One and hit the beach squarely on "the bird's beak." PFC Moore tried to drive his LVT over the 5-foot seawall, but the vehicle stalled in a vertical position while Japanese machine guns riddled troops inside. PFC Moore reached for his rifle and found it shot in half. He later recalled what happened next on the LVT:

The sergeant stood up and yelled, 'everybody out!' but as soon as the words left his mouth, machine-gun bullets ripped the top of his head off.

PFC Moore and a handful of others escaped the LVT and destroyed two machine-gun positions a few yards away. All would either be killed or injured during the assault . Few of the LVTs could negotiate the 5-foot seawall. While the LVTs stalled on the beach, they were vulnerable to howitzer and mortar fire, as well as hand grenades thrown into the troop compartments by Japanese troops on the other side of the barrier.

One crew chief of the vehicle, Cpl. Spillane, a baseball prospect with the St. Louis Cardinals before the war, caught two Japanese grenades barehanded in midair and tossed them back over the wall. He caught a third grenade that exploded in his hand and fatally wounded him.

MAELSTROM ON BETIO

WAVES Two and Three of the LVT-2s were protected by a 3/8 inch boilerplate hastily installed in Samoa. These waves suffered even more intense fire. The large-caliber anti-boat Japanese guns destroyed several of the LVT-2s. Machine gunner PFC Baird, aboard one of the embattled LVTs, recounted what he saw:

> *After we were 100 yards in, the enemy fire was awful damn intense and only getting worse. They were knocking us out left and right. A tractor would get hit, stop, and burst into flames. Men jumped out like torches.*

PFC Baird's LVT was hit by a shell and killed many of the troops. He recalled:

> *I grabbed my carbine and an ammunition box. I stepped over a couple fellas lying there dead and put my hand on the side to roll*

over into the water. I didn't want to put my head up. The bullets poured over us like a sheet of rain.

The LVTs executed the assault according to Gen. Smith's expectations. Eight out of the eighty-seven vehicles in the first three waves were lost in the assault. Fifteen others were so damaged and riddled with holes that they sank when reaching deep water while seeking to shuttle more troops to shore. Within ten minutes, the LVTs landed over 1,500 Marines on Betio's north shore. While a brilliant start to the operation, the problem was sustaining the momentum of the assault. The neap tide predictions were accurate. No landing craft could cross that reef on D-Day.

Col. Shoup hoped that enough LVTs would survive to permit a wholesale transfer operation with the boats along the edge of the reef. It would not work. The LVTs suffered more casualties. Several vehicles, afloat for only five hours, ran out of gas. Others needed to be used immediately for the evacuation of wounded Marines. The already flawed communications deteriorated even more as the radio sets suffered water damage from enemy fire. The surviving LVTs continued on. But after 1015, most troops had waded ashore from the reef, crossing distances of 1,000 yards, under well-aimed fire. The Marines of the 3/2 were walloped on Red Beach One. Company K suffered casualties from the stronghold on the left. Company I crossed the seawall but paid a high price—losing their company commander before he could even debark from his LVT. Both units lost more than half of their men within the first two hours.

Major Michael Ryan's Company L was forced to wade ashore when their boats grounded on the reef, taking over 35% casualties. Maj. Ryan spotted one lone trooper through the fire and smoke scrambling over a parapet on the beach to the right, marking a new landing point. When Company L finally reached the shore, Maj. Ryan looked back over his shoulder, and all he could see were heads with rifles held over them. He ordered his men to make as small of a target as possible. Ryan assembled the various stragglers in a sheltered area along Green Beach.

In the fourth wave, Major Schoettel remained in his boat with the remnants of his Marines. He was convinced that his landing team had been destroyed beyond relief. He had no contact with Major Ryan. Schoettel received fragmented reports that seventeen of his thirty-seven officers were combat ineffective casualties.

In the center, the 2/2 Marines were thumped hard coming ashore. The Japanese strong point in the re-entrant between the two beaches created turmoil among the Marines scrambling over the sides of their stalled and beached LVTs. Five out of six of Company E's officers were killed. Company F took 50% casualties getting ashore and negotiating the seawall to seize a foothold. Company G barely clung to a crowded stretch of beach along the seawall in the middle. Two infantry platoons and two machine gun platoons were driven away from their beach. They were forced to land on Red Beach One, joining "Major Ryan's orphans."

When Lieutenant Colonel Amey's boat ran against the reef, he hailed a passing LVTs for a transfer. After that, LtCol. Amey's LVT became hung up on a barbed wire obstacle several hundred yards off Red Beach Two. Amey drew his pistol and shouted for his men to follow him into the water. As he got closer to the beach, LtCol. Amey turned to encourage his men:

Come on! These bastards can't beat us.

A machine gun fire burst hit him in the throat—killing

him instantly. His XO, Major Rice, and another LVT landed far to the west behind Major Ryan. Lieutenant Colonel Walter Jordan was the senior officer present with the 2/2. He was one of the several observers from the 4th Marine Division, and only one of a handful of survivors from LtCol. Amey's LVT.

LtCol. Jordan did what any Marine would do under the circumstances: he took command. Jordan tried to rebuild the pieces of the landing team into a cohesive fighting force.

The only amphibious assault unit that got ashore without significant casualties was the 2/8 on Red Beach Three, east of the pier. This good fortune was attributed to the continued direct fire support the 2/8 received, throughout its run to the beach, from the two destroyers in the lagoon. The fire support from the two ships provided a preliminary fire from such a short-range. It kept the Japanese defenders on the island's eastern edge buttoned up. As a result, the 2/8 only suffered less than 25% casualties in the first three LVT waves. Company E made a significant penetration by crossing the barricade and the taxiway. Still, five of its six officers were shot down in the first ten minutes ashore. The 2/8 was fighting against one of the most sophisticated defensive positions on the islands. These fortifications to their left flank would keep the Marines boxed in for the next forty-eight hours.

Major "Jim" Crowe was the commander of the 2/8 Marines. A former enlisted man, gunner, distinguished rifleman, and star football player, he was a tower of strength through the battle. He carried a combat shotgun cradled in his arm. With his trademark red mustache, he exuded professionalism and confidence that were sorely needed on Betio that day. Maj. Crowe ordered the coxswain of his Higgins boat to "put the god damn boat in." The Higgins boat hit the reef at high speed, sending Marines sprawling. Crowe quickly recovered and ordered his men over the sides and then led them through hundreds of yards of shallow water. They reached the shore intact only four minutes behind the last wave of LVTs.

Crowe was accompanied by a combat photographer who recalled the major clenching a cigar in his teeth and standing upright, growling at his men:

Look, these sons of bitches can't hit me. Why do you think they can hit you? Get your asses moving. Go!

Red Beach Three was in capable hands.

By 0945 on Betio, Maj. Crowe was well-established, with a penetration to the airfield. A distinct gap existed between the 2/8 and the survivors of 2/2 in small clusters along Red Beach Two under LtCol. Jordan's command. It was a dangerous gap because of the Japanese fortifications between Beaches One and Two. Only a few members of 3/2 on the left flank and a growing collection of Marines under Maj. Ryan were on Green Beach.

Major Schoettel was floating beyond the reef. Col. Shoup was likewise in a Higgins boat, but starting his move toward the beach. Other Marines waded ashore under increasing enemy fire. The tanks were forced to unload from the LCMs at the reef's edge, searching for recon teams to lead them ashore.

Communications were a nightmare. The TBX radios of Crowe, Shoup, and Schoettel were still operational. But there was either dead silence or complete havoc on the command nets. No one on the flagship knew of Maj. Ryan's successful debark on the western end, or of LtCol. Amey's death and LtCol. Jordan's assumption of command. An early report from an unknown source flashed over the command nets:

Have landed. Unusually heavy opposition. Casualties 70%. Can't hold.

Col. Shoup ordered the 1/2 regimental reserve to land on Red Beach Two and work west. This would take time because the men were still awaiting orders at the line of departure, but all were waiting embarked in boats. Col. Shoup assembled enough LVTs to transport companies A and B. The 3rd Infantry Company and the Weapons Company had yet to wade ashore through this chaotic assault. Most of the LVTs were destroyed en route by anti-boat guns. Japanese gunners now had the range down pat. Five vehicles were driven away by the intense fire and landed west at Maj. Ryan's position, giving him another 113 troops to add to Green Beach.

The rest of companies A and B stormed ashore and penetrated several hundred feet, expanding the perimeter. Other troops sought refuge along the pier and tried to commandeer a passing LVT. Many of the regimental reserve 1/2 troops did not complete the landing until the following morning. It was typical for an LVT driver and his gunners to be shot down by enemy machine gun fire. The surviving crewmen would get the stranded vehicle started again, but only in reverse. The vehicle would back wildly through the entire impact zone before breaking down again, causing several men to not reach the shore until sunset.

Naval commanders received their first clear signal that things were going wrong on the beach when a derelict LVT chugged astern with no one at the controls. They dispatched a boat to retrieve the vehicle and discovered three dead Marines aboard the LVT. Their bodies were brought on board and buried with full honors at sea. These were the first of hundreds of men consigned to the deep because of the maelstrom on Betio.

After the communications were restored on the *Maryland,* Gen. Smith tried to make sense of the conflicting and intermittent messages coming in through the ship's command net. At 1036 Gen. Smith reported to the V Amphibious Corps:

Successful landing on beaches Red Two and Three. Toehold on Red One. And committing one LT from division reserved. Still encountering strong resistance.

Col. Shoup was trying to navigate getting ashore. When his Higgins boat was stopped at the reef, he transferred into a passing LVT. He joined Colonel Evans Carlson, a legend for his exploits on Guadalcanal and Makin. He took command of the 1/10 Artillery detachment. Their LVT made three attempts to land—each time the enemy fire was too intense. On the third attempt, the vehicle was hit and disabled. Col. Shoup took a painful shell fragment wound in his leg but led his men out of the LVT and into the fight. He stood in waist-deep water surrounded by thousands of dead fish and floating bodies. Shoup manned his radio and tried desperately to get organized combat units ashore to sway the fight's balance.

Col. Shoup had hoped that the Sherman tanks could break the gridlock. This was the combat debut of the Marine Corps' medium tanks but was discouraging on D-Day. The 2nd Marine Division did not understand how to employ tanks against fortified positions. When four Shermans reached Red Beach Three, later in the morning, Maj. Crowe waved them forward with orders to knock out all enemy positions. The tank crews, who were buttoned up under fire, were practically blind in their tanks. With no accompanying infantry, they were destroyed one by one. Some were knocked out by the Japanese 75mm guns, while others were damaged by friendly fire from American dive bombers.

Six other Shermans that tried to land on Red Beach One were preceded by a dismounted guide to warn off underwater shell craters. These guides were shot down every few minutes by Japanese marksmen. Each time, another volunteer would step forward to continue the movement. Combat engineers had blown a hole in the seawall for the tanks to pass through, but the way was blocked with wounded and dead Marines. Rather than run over their fellow Marines, the tank commander reversed his column and went around toward a second opening blasted in the seawall.

While the Shermans operated in murky, chaotic waters, four tanks foundered in shell holes on the detour. Inland on the beach, one of the surviving Sherman's engaged a Japanese light tank. The medium American tank demolished its small opponent, but not before the doomed Japanese tank released one final 37mm round—a phenomenal shot—right down the barrel of the Sherman.

RED BEACH TWO

By THE END of the day, only two of the fourteen Sherman tanks were still operational. Maintenance crews worked desperately to retrieve a third tank, *Cecilia*, on Green Beach for Maj. Ryan. Japanese gunners sank all four of the LCMs transporting the light tanks into the battle before the boats even reached the reef. The tank battalion commander, Colonel Swenceski, was assumed killed in action while wading ashore. He was severely wounded but survived by crawling on top of a pile of dead bodies to keep from drowning until he was discovered the next day.

Col. Shoup sent a message to the flagship at 1045 on D-Day voicing his frustration:

Our tanks no good. Stiff resistance, need half-tracks.

The regimental weapons company's half-tracks with their 75mm guns fared no better getting ashore than any other combat units that morning. One half-track was sunk in its LCM transport by long-range artillery fire before reaching the reef. A second half-track ran the entire gauntlet but got stuck in the loose sand at the water's edge and was destroyed. The situation was now critical.

Individual courage and initiative inspired the scattered remnants throughout the chaos along the exposed beachhead. Staff Sergeant Bordelon was a combat engineer attached to the 2/2. After a Japanese shell disabled his LVT and killed most of the troops en route to the beach, Bordelon rallied the survivors and led them ashore on Red Beach Two. He stopped only long enough to prepare explosive charges. He knocked out two Japanese positions that had been firing on the assault waves. After attacking a third emplacement, he was hit by machine-gun fire but refused medical help and continued fighting. SSgt. Bordelon bolted back into the water and rescued a wounded Marine calling for help. As more intense fire opened up from another enemy position, Bordelon prepared one final demolition package and charged the

Japanese gun position in a frontal assault. This is where his luck ran out. He was shot and killed. He later became the first of four men in the 2nd Marine Division to be awarded the Medal of Honor.

In another instance, Sgt. Roy Johnson single-handedly attacked a Japanese tank. He scrambled to the turret and dropped a grenade inside while sitting on the hatch, waiting for the detonation. Sgt. Johnson survived this but was later killed in the fighting on Betio. In the 76 hour battle, he was one of the 217 Marine sergeants to be wounded or killed.

A captain on Red Beach Three, who was shot through both arms and legs, sent a message to Maj. Crowe apologizing for letting him down.

Maj. Ryan later recalled a wounded Sgt., who he'd never seen before, limping up to him and asking where he was needed most.

PFC Moore, who was earlier disarmed and wounded, trying to drive "My Dolores" over the seawall, carried ammo to the machine gun crews for the rest of the day until he was evacuated to one of the transports.

Other brave Marines retrieved a pair of 37mm antitank guns from a sunken landing craft. They manhandled them across several hundred yards under terrifying enemy fire. They dragged them across the beach to the seawall. While two Japanese tanks approached the beachheads, the Marines lifted the 900-pound antitank guns on top of the seawall. They calmly loaded, aimed, and fired. Knocking out one of the Japanese tanks at close range and chasing off the other.

Robert Sherrod was an experienced war correspondent for *Time* magazine. The landing on D-Day at Betio was the most frightening experience of his life. Sherrod accompanied Marines from the fourth wave of 2/2 and tried to wade ashore on Red Beach Two. In his own words:

No sooner did we hit the water than the Japanese machine guns really opened up on us. It was so painfully slow, we waded in such deep water. We had 700 yards to walk slowly into direct machine-gun fire, looming into larger targets as we rose onto the higher ground. I was so scared, more than I'd ever been before. Those who weren't hit would always remember how the machine-gun bullets hissed into the water, inches to the right, inches to the left.

Col. Shoup moved toward the beach parallel to the pier. He ordered Major Ruud's 3/8 Marines to land on Red Beach Three—east of the pier. There were now no organized LVT units to transport the reserve battalion to the fight. Maj. Ruud was ordered to approach as near as he could to the landing boats and then wade the remaining distance into shore. Ruud received his orders from Col. Shoup at 1104. While the two officers were never more than a mile apart from each other for the next six hours, they could not communicate.

Maj. Ruud divided his landing team into seven waves. Once the boats approached, the reef confusion began. The Japanese zeroed their anti-boat guns on the landing craft with fearsome accuracy. They scored several direct hits as the bow ramp dropped. A distinct *clang* from an impacting shell would signal a split second before the explosion. SSgt. Hatch watching from the beach later recalled:

It happened at least a dozen times. The boat was blown completely out of the water and smashed bodies all over the place. I watched a Jap shell hit a landing craft directly that brought many Marines ashore. The explosion was horrific, and parts of the boat flew in all directions.

Navy coxswains watching the slaughter directly ahead stopped their boats seaward of the reef and ordered troops to debark. Many Marines loaded with extra ammunition or radios instantly sank into the deep water—many drowned. The reward for the troops whose coxswains made it into the reef was less sanguine. They waded through 600 yards of withering crossfire. Heavier, by far, than what the first assault waves experienced at H-Hour. The first wave slaughter of companies L and K was terrible. Over 70% fell while attempting to reach the beach.

Col. Shoup and his party frantically waved to groups of Marines to seek the pier's protection. While many did, several NCOs and officers had been hit, making the stragglers disorganized. The pier was a questionable shelter; it received sniper fire, and intermittent machine-gun fire from both sides. Col. Shoup was struck in nine places. A bullet came close to penetrating his bull-like neck. His runner crouching behind him was shot between the eyes by a Japanese sniper.

The commander of the 3/8 Weapons Company, Captain Carl Hoffman, fared no better getting ashore than the infantry companies ahead. His landing craft took a direct hit from a Japanese mortar, and he lost six or eight men right there. Capt. Hoffman's Marines veered toward the peer and then waded toward shore. Maj. Ruud was unable to contact Col. Shoup. And instead radioed his regimental commander, Colonel Elmer Hall:

Third wave landed on Red Beach Three. Practically wiped out. Fourth wave landed but only a few Marines ashore.

Col. Hall was in a small boat near the line of departure, unable to respond. General Hermle, Assistant Division Commander, intervened with this message:

Stay where you are or retreat out of gun range.

This only added to the confusion. Maj. Ruud did not reach the pier until late afternoon. At 1730 he was able to lead what was left of his men ashore.

Many Marines did not straggle in until the following day. Col. Shoup dispatched what was left of the 3/8 to support Maj. Crowe's besieged 2/8. Other Marines were used to plug the gap between the 2/8 and the combined troops of the 2/2 and the 1/2.

When Col. Shoup finally reached Betio and established his command post. He was fifty yards in from the pier along the blindside of a Japanese occupied bunker. Shoup posted guards to keep the enemy from launching any attacks. Still, the site's approaches were exposed, just like any other place on the flat island. Over twenty messengers were shot while bearing dispatches to and from Col. Shoup.

Combat photographer Sherrod crawled to look out at the exposed water on both sides of the pier. He counted over fifty disabled LVTs, boats, and tanks.

Col. Shoup admitted to him, "We need more men. We're in a tight spot." The situation did not look good.

Col. Shoup's first order of business after reaching dry ground was to seek updated reports from his landing team commanders. Tactical communications were worse now than they had been during the morning assault. Col. Shoup still had no contact with any troops on Red Beach One, nor could he raise Gen. Smith on *Maryland*. A messenger arrived with a report from 2/2:

All communications out except runners. We need help. Situation bad. CO killed. No word from E Company.

Col. Shoup found LtCol. Jordan and ordered him to take command of the 2/2. Shoup reinforced him with elements of the 1/2 and 3/8. He gave Jordan an hour to organize and rearm the assorted attachments. Shoup then ordered him to proceed inland to attack the airstrip and expand the beachhead. Col. Shoup then ordered Col. Carlson to hitch a ride to the *Maryland* and inform Gen. Smith of the situation personally. He told Col. Carlson to tell the general, "We're going to stick it out and fight."

Carlson departed immediately. But because of the hazards and confusion between the line of departure and the beach, he did not reach the flagship with his message until 1800.

FOG OF WAR

COL. SHOUP FOCUSED his attention on the critical matters of resupply. Beyond the pier were over a hundred small craft that circled aimlessly. They carried assorted supplies from cargo and transport ships. They unloaded as quickly as they could in compliance with Adm. Nimitz's orders of "Get the hell in and then get the hell out."

The unorganized unloading hindered the fight ashore. Shoup was not sure of which boat held what supplies. He sent word that only the most critical supplies were to be sent to the pier: LVT fuel, ammunition, water, blood plasma, and more radios. The naval gunfire support since the landing was terrific, but it was time for the Marines to bring their own artillery to the beachhead. The original plan of landing the 1/10 Marines at Red Beach One was no longer practical.

Shoup conferred with Lieutenant Colonel Presley Rixey and agreed to land on Red Beach Two's left flank with the 75mm howitzers. These expeditionary guns would be broken down and manhandled ashore. LtCol. Rixey had seen close up what happened when the 3/8 tried to wade ashore from the reef. He went after the last few LVTs. There were only enough operational vehicles for two sections of Batteries A and B. In the confusion, three Battery C sections followed the LVTs toward the shore in their open boats. Luck smiled on the artillerymen. The LVTs landed with intact guns in the late afternoon. When the trailing boats were hung up on the reef, Marines dragged the heavy components through the bullet swept waters to the pier and made it ashore by twilight. There was now close-in fire support available at dawn.

Gen. Julian Smith knew little of what was happening. He continued trying to piece together the tactical situation onshore. Smith received reports from staff officers afloat and in float planes. He decided the situation in the early afternoon was in desperate straits.

Although he had elements of five infantry battalions ashore, their toehold was unstable. Gen. Smith decided the gap between Red Beach One and Red Beach Two had not been closed. And that the left flank on Red Beach Three was not secure. Smith assumed that Col. Shoup was still alive and in command, but he could not afford to gamble. Over the next few hours, the commanding general did his best to influence all-action ashore from the flagship. Smith's first step was to send a radio message to Gen. Holland Smith. He requested the use of the 6th Marines to division control because the situation was in doubt. He also ordered his last remaining landing team, 1/8 Marines, to the line of departure. Gen. Julian Smith reorganized another emergency division composed of engineers, artillery, and service troop units.

Gen. Julian Smith ordered Gen. Hermle to proceed to the end of the pier and assess the situation and report back. Hermle took his small staff and promptly debarked from the *Monrovia* headed toward the smoking island—but the trip took four hours. During this time, Gen. Julian Smith received a message from Maj. Schoettel, still afloat seaward at the reef:

Command post located on back of Red Beach One. Situation as before. Lost all contact with assault elements.

Gen. Smith replied:

Land at any cost. Regain control of your battalion and continue to attack.

Maj. Schoettel reached the beach at sunset. It was well into the next day before he could work west and consolidate the scattered Marines. Gen. Smith received authorization to take control of the 6th Marines at 1525. Smith now had four battalions of landing teams available at his disposal. The question was how to feed them into the fight without getting them annihilated like Maj. Ruud's experience trying to land the 3/8.

Again, Gen. Smith's communications failed him. At 1740 he received a message from Hermle that he had reached the pier and was under fire. Ten minutes later, Smith ordered Hermle to take command of all forces onshore. Hermle never received these orders. Gen. Smith did not know his message failed to get through, and Hermle remained at the pier sending runners to Col. Shoup, who told him to "Get the hell out from underneath that pier." They tried with little success to unscrew the two-way movement of casualties and supplies to shore.

Throughout the long day, Col. Hall and his staff languished in their Higgins boats next to the 1/8 waiting at the line of departure. They were wet, cramped, hungry, and tired with many seasick Marines. Later in the afternoon, Gen. Smith ordered Hall to land all of his remaining units on the beach on the northeast tip of the island and work west toward Col. Shoup's ragged lines. This was extremely risky. Gen. Smith's primary concern was that the Japanese would counterattack from the eastern tail of the island against his left flank. Once he had the 6th Marines, Gen. Smith later admitted he would've sacrificed a battalion landing team if it meant saving the landing force from being overrun by a Japanese counterattack during the night.

Luckily, Hall never received this message from Gen. Smith. Later that afternoon, a float plane reported to Smith that a unit crossed the departure line and headed for the left flank of Red Beach Two. Gen. Smith assumed it was Hall going to the wrong beach. But this was the beginning of Rixey's artillerymen moving ashore. The 8th Marines spent the night in their boats waiting for orders. Gen. Smith did not discover this until early the next morning.

On Betio, Maj. Ryan reported to Col. Shoup that several hundred Marines and two tanks had penetrated over 500 yards beyond Red Beach One on the island's western end. This was now the most successful progress of the day and welcome news to Col. Shoup, because he'd feared the worst. He'd assumed Schoettel's companies and all other strays who'd veered in that direction were wiped out. This was more news that Col. Shoup could not convey to Gen. Smith.

Maj. Ryan's troops were effective on the western end. They learned how to best operate the medium tanks and carved out a substantial beachhead. They overran several Japanese pillboxes and turrets. Aside from the tanks, Maj. Ryan's men had only infantry weapons. They had no demolitions or flamethrowers. Maj. Ryan new from his earlier experiences fighting in the Solomons that positions reduced by only grenades could come alive again. He decided by late afternoon to pull back his thin lines and consolidate. In his words:

I was convinced that without any flamethrowers or explosives to clean them out, we needed to pull back . . . to a perimeter that could be defended against a counterattack by Japanese troops still hidden in the bunkers.

The fundamental choice by Marines on Betio was whether to stay put on the beach or try and crawl over the seawall to fight inland. Much of the day, the fire came across the coconut logs so intensely that a man could lift his hand and get it shot off. Late on D-Day, many Marines were too demoralized to advance. Major Ravoth Tompkins brought messages from Gen. Hermle to Col. Shoup. Tompkins arrived on Red Beach Two at the foot of the pier at dusk on D-Day. He was appalled at the sight of so many Marine stragglers. Tompkins wondered why the Japanese didn't just use mortars on the first night. He later reported that Marines lying on the beach were so thick you couldn't walk through them.

The conditions on Red Beach One were congested as well, but there was a difference. Maj. Crowe was everywhere, "as cool as icebox lettuce." There weren't any stragglers. Maj. Crowe fed small groups of Marines into the lines, reinforcing his precarious hold on the left flank. Capt. Hoffman of the 3/8 Marines welcomed the integration of Crowe's 2/8 Marines. Hoffman needed help as darkness fell. He recalled:

There we were, toes in the water, casualties everywhere, dead and wounded all around us. But finally, a few Marines started to inch forward, a yard here, a yard there.

It was enough, Hoffman could see well enough to call in naval gunfire support. His men dug in for the night. To the west of Maj. Crowe's lines, and inland from Col. Shoup's command post, was Company B of the 1/2. They had settled in for the expected counterattack. Scattered in the bloody landing at midday, Company B had men from 12 to 14 different units, including sailors, who swam ashore from sinking boats. These men were all well-armed and no longer stragglers.

Of the 5,000 Marines that stormed the beaches of Betio on D-Day, 1,500 of them were missing, dead, or wounded by nightfall. The survivors held only a quarter of a square mile of coral and sand. Col. Shoup later described the location of his beachhead lines the night of D-Day as "a stock market graph." The Marines went to ground in the best fighting positions they could secure, whether in inland shell holes or along the splintered seawall. Despite the defensive positions and scrambled units, the fire discipline of the Marines was superb. The troops shared a grim confidence. They'd already faced the worst in getting ashore. They were ready for any *banzai* charges in the dark.

Gen. Smith on the *Maryland* was concerned. He recalled:

This was the crisis of the battle. Three-fourths of the island was in enemy hands. A concerted Japanese counterattack would've driven us into the sea.

Smith reported up his chain of command to Admirals Spruance, Turner, and Nimitz that the issue still remained in doubt. Adm. Spruance's staff began drafting plans for an emergency evacuation of the landing force.

Throughout the night of D-Day, the main struggle was Shoup and Hermle's attempt to try and advise Gen. Smith of the best place to land the reserves the following morning. Gen. Smith was astonished to learn at 0200, that Col. Hall was not ashore but still at the line of departure awaiting orders. Smith again ordered combat team eight to land on the eastern tip of the island at 0900 on D+1.

Gen. Hermle finally caught a boat back to one of the destroyers. He relayed Shoup's request to land reinforcements on Red Beach Two. Gen. Smith modified Col. Hall's orders. Smith ordered Hermle back to the flagship, irked at his assistant for not getting ashore and taking command. In the end, Gen. Hermle had done Smith a useful service by relaying the advice from Col. Shoup. As much as the 8th Marines would bleed in the next morning's assault, a landing on the island's eastern end would have been a disaster. Reconnaissance after the battle discovered those beaches to be the most intensely mined on the entire island.

D+1 AT BETIO

THE TACTICAL SITUATION on Betio was perilous for most of the second day. During the morning, the Marines paid in blood for every attempt to land reserves or advance the ragged beachheads. Tarawa's beaches were gruesome and filled with the dead and dying. Col. Shoup surveyed the beach at first light and was horrified. In his own words:

It was a dreadful sight, bodies drifted slowly in the water just off the beach. The stench of dead bodies covered the island like a cloud.

The smell wafted out a bad omen to the line of departure for the 1/8 Marines getting ready to start their run into the beach. With an imperfect knowledge of the scattered forces and his faulty communications, Col. Shoup ordered each landing team commander to attack. LtCol. Jordan would take the south coast. Rudd and Crowe were to reduce the Japanese strongholds to their left and front. Maj. Ryan was to take all of Green Beach.

Col. Shoup's predawn request to Gen. Smith relayed a specific landing of the 1/8 on Red Beach Two close to the pier. Unfortunately, this critical component of Col. Shoup's request did not survive the communications route to Gen. Smith. The commanding general ordered Major Lawrence C. Hays Jr. and Col. Hall to land on Red Beach Two at 0615. Hays and Hall were oblivious of the situation ashore and assumed that the 1/8 would make a covered landing.

The Marines of the 1/8 had spent eighteen hours in the embarked Higgins boats, making endless circles through the night. The troops cheered when the boats finally made their turn toward the beach.

Things went wrong quickly. The tides failed to provide enough water for the boats to cross the reef. Hays' men debarked over the obstacle and started the 500-yard trek to shore. Dangerously far to the right flank and within the zone of Japanese guns firing from the strong re-entrant point. They were in the worst place they could be. Japanese gunners began an unrelenting fire. Japanese snipers raked the Marines from the disabled LVTs they had infiltrated during the night. Multiple machine guns opened up on the waiting troops from every beached interisland schooner at the reef's edge. Hays' men fell at every turn.

The Marines tried to stop the slaughter. Col. Shoup called for naval gunfire support. Two 75mm howitzers protected by a sand berm, erected from a Seabee bulldozer, fired at the blockhouses at the Red Beach One/Two border using delayed fuses in high explosive shells. A squadron of F4F Wildcats attacked the Japanese defenders with machine guns and bombs. While these measures helped, the Japanese had caught the Marines in a withering crossfire.

Correspondent Sherrod watched this bloodbath in horror. In an hour, Sherrod counted at least two hundred bodies that did not move on the dry flats. He recalled:

One boat blows up, then another. The survivors start to swim for shore, but machine-gun bullets dot the water all around them. Far worse today than yesterday.

First Lieutenant Dean Ladd jumped into the water from his boat and was shot in the stomach. He recalled the troops' strict orders to not stop for the wounded and expected to die on the spot. One of his riflemen, PFC Sullivan, ignored the orders and saved his lieutenant's life. Ladd's rifle platoon suffered twenty-four casualties during the ship to shore assault.

First Lieutenant Frank Plant, the air liaison officer, was with Maj. Hays in the command Higgins boat. After the call, the craft slammed into the reef, Maj. Hays shouted for the men to debark. As he jumped in the water, the troops that followed him were cut down by the murderous fire. Lieut. Plant helped to pull the wounded back into the boat. He later wrote that the water all around him was colored purple with blood. As he hurriedly caught up with Maj. Hays, he was terrified at the sudden appearance of what he thought were Japanese fighters roaring toward him. But they were the Navy Wildcats screaming in to attack the Japanese. The pilots were excited but inconsistent. While one bomb hit the Japanese defenders, others missed by over 200 yards and contributed to the dying Marines' chaos. An angry Col. Shoup came on the radio:

Stop strafing. Bombs hitting our own troops.

It was only sheer courage of the survivors that got them ashore under such a hellish crossfire. Maj. Hays reported to Shoup at 0800 with only half of his landing team. He had taken over three hundred casualties while other men were missing and scattered along the beach and pier. His unit had lost all of its heavy weapons, demolitions, and flamethrowers. Col. Shoup directed Hays to attack west. Both men knew that small arms and courage would not overtake the Japanese in their fortified positions.

The combined forces of Majors Rudd in Crowe on Red Beach Three were full of fight and had sufficient weapons. Their left flank was flush against three large Japanese bunkers, each mutually supporting each other and unassailable. The stubby pier slightly to the east of the main pier turned into a bloody no-man's-land as the two sides fought for possession. Learning from the mistakes of D-Day, Maj. Crowe ensured his one surviving Sherman was always accompanied by infantry.

Rudd and Crowe benefited from the intense air support and naval gunfire on their left flank. Maj. Crowe was later to write that he was unimpressed with the aviators' effectiveness and accuracy, and that the aircraft never did that much good. But he was enthusiastic about the naval guns:

I had the three destroyers supporting me: the Ringgold, the Daschle, and the Anderson. Anything I asked for, I got. I authorized a direct fire from one of the destroyers in the lagoon at a command bunker only 50 yards ahead of us during the fight. They slammed the fire in there, and you could see arms and legs and everything just go up like that.

LtCol. Jordan managed to get some of his troops across the fire-swept airstrip inland from Red Beach Two all the way to the southern coast—making a significant penetration. Their toehold was precarious, and his Marines suffered heavy casualties. He recalled that he could not see the Japanese. Still, the fire came from every direction when Jordan lost contact with his lead elements. Col. Shoup ordered him across the island to reestablish command. Jordan did so at a significant hazard to himself. By the time his reinforcements arrived, LtCol. Jordan had only fifty men, who could be accounted for, from his landing team's 2/2 rifle companies. The colonel organized and supplied these men to the best of his abilities. Then, at Shoup's orders, he merged them with the reinforcements and stepped back into his original role as an observer.

SCOUT SNIPER PLATOON

THE HEROICS of the 2nd Marines Scout Sniper Platoon had been spectacular from the start, when they led the assault on the pier, just before H-Hour. 1stLt. Hawkins was an example of having a cool disregard for danger in every tactical situation.

While he displayed superhuman bravery, it would not protect him in the turmoil. A Japanese shell had wounded him on D-Day, and he shook off any attempts to treat his injuries. At dawn on D+1, he led his men in a series of attacks on Japanese strong points. Hawkins crawled up to a pillbox, fired his weapon point-blank through the gun ports, and threw grenades inside to finish the job. He was shot in the chest but continued to attack and took out three more pillboxes personally. Just after that, a Japanese shell tore him apart.

The division mourned his death, and he was awarded the Medal of Honor posthumously. Col. Shoup recalled:

It's not often that you can credit a first lieutenant with winning a battle, but Lieut. Hawkins came as near to it as any man possibly could have.

It was now up to Maj. Ryan and his makeshift battalion on the western side of Betio to make the most considerable contribution to winning the battle. Ryan's fortunes were enhanced by three developments during the night.

1. The Japanese did not counterattack his thin lines.
2. Seabees repaired his medium tank, *Cecilia*.
3. The arrival of a naval gunfire spotter, Lieutenant Thomas Green, with a fully functional radio.

Ryan organized a coordinated attack against the Japanese pillboxes, gun emplacements, and rifle pits concentrated on the island's southwestern corner. Slowed by communication failures, Ryan could talk to the fire support ships but not Col. Shoup. It took hours for his runners to negotiate the fire gauntlet and return with answers from Shoup's CP.

Ryan's first message to Shoup revealed his attack plans but was delayed because Col. Shoup called in an airstrike. After two more runners, the airstrike was canceled, and Ryan called in a naval gunfire strike on the southwest targets. Two of the destroyers in the lagoon responded accurately and promptly. Maj. Ryan launched a coordinated tank/infantry assault at 1120. In less than an hour, his makeshift force had seized all of Green Beach and was ready to move eastward toward the airfield and attack.

The communications were still awful. Maj. Ryan twice reported that the southern end of Green Beach was intensely mined. That message reached no higher headquarters. Gen. Smith on the *Maryland* did not receive any direct word of Maj.

Ryan's successes. Smith was delighted when he learned he could land reinforcements on the covered beach and keep the unit integrity intact.

Gen. Smith conferred with Colonel Holmes, commander of the 6th Marines, as to the best way of getting the fresh combat teams into the fight. Due to the heavy casualties taken by Hays' battalion on Red Beach Two, Smith reassessed his landing on an unknown eastern end of the island. Maj. Ryan's good news quickly solved this problem. Smith ordered Holmes to land one of his battalions by rubber raft on Green Beach and have the second landing team boated in and prepared to wade ashore in support.

Gen. Smith received reports that the Japanese troops were retreating from the eastern end of Betio by wading across to the next islet: Bairiki. The Marines did not want to fight the same deadly enemy twice. Holmes ordered the 2/6 to land on Bairiki and "seal the back door." The 1/6 was ordered to land on Green Beach by rubber boat. The 3/6 was held in reserve and prepared to land at any assigned spot, probably Green Beach. Gen. Smith ordered the light tanks of Company B to land on Green Beach, supporting the 6th Marines.

These tactical plans took much longer to execute than envisioned. The 1/6 was waiting and ready to debark when their ship *Feland* was ordered underway because of a submarine threat. It would be hours before the *Feland* could return close enough to Betio and launch the rubber boats and the Higgins tow craft. These light tanks were now among the few critical items not loaded into the transports because they were in the very bottom of the cargo holds. During the first thirty-five hours of the landing, poor loading practices had further scrambled all supplies and equipment into intervening decks. It would take hours to clear the tanks and get them loaded on board.

Frustrated by the long delays, Shoup sent a message at 1345, asking for flamethrowers. He desperately wanted the

1/6 ashore to begin their attack. Col. Shoup, and his small staff were continually frustrated by logistical support problems. His team organized men to strip the dead of first-aid pouches, canteens, and ammunition. He also organized a shore party to create a false beachhead at the end of the pier.

The primary control officer onboard the minesweeper, *Pursuit*, Captain McGovern, eventually brought order by taking strict control of all unloading supplies. He used the surviving LVTs to keep the shuttle of casualties moving seaward and bring all critical items from the pier head to the beach.

This task was completed by men who hadn't slept in days and worked under constant enemy fire.

TIDE OF BATTLE

THE HANDLING of casualties was the most pressing logistical problem on D+1. The 2nd Marine Division was served heroically by its Navy corpsmen and doctors. Over ninety of these medical specialists were casualties in the onshore fighting.

Lieutenant Herman Brukhardt established an emergency room in a captured Japanese bunker. Some of the former occupants came to life, firing their rifles more than once. But, in over thirty-six hours and under brutal conditions, Lieut. Brukhardt treated 126 wounded men, only losing four.

The casualties were at first evacuated to the far off troopships. Because a long journey was so dangerous and wasteful of the few available LVTs or Higgins boats, the Marines began to deliver casualties to the destroyer *Ringgold* in the lagoon. Even though her sickbay had been destroyed by a 5-inch Japanese shell on D-Day, the destroyer still actively fired in support missions and accepted dozens of casualties.

Adm. Hill dispatched the troopship, *Doyen*, into the lagoon early on D+1 to be used as a primary critical receiving ship. Lieutenant Commander Oliver led a surgical team of five men with recent combat experience from the Aleutian Islands.

In three days, Oliver's team treated over 550 wounded Marines. In his own words:

> *We'd run out of sodium pentathol and had to use ether. If a bomb would've hit us, Doyen would have blown off the face of the planet.*

The Navy chaplains were also hard at work wherever the Marines were fighting onshore. They had heartbreaking work: administering last rites to the dying, consoling the wounded, and praying for the souls of the dead before the bulldozer came to cover the bodies from the unforgiving tropical sun.

The tide of battle now shifted toward the Americans by the middle of the afternoon on D+1. While the fighting was still intense, and Japanese fire deadly, the surviving Marines were now moving. No longer gridlocked in dangerous toeholds, LtCol. Rixey's howitzers made a new definition of close-in fire support. Supplies of fresh water and ammunition were improved. Morale was rising. The troops knew the 6th Marines would come in soon. LtCol. Rixey later wrote:

> *I thought up until 1300 today it was touch and go, after that I knew we would win.*

Despair spread among the Japanese defenders. While they had shot down Marines at every turn they could—another would appear in his place: rifle blazing, well supported by naval and artillery guns. The great Japanese *Yogaki Plan* was a failure. Only a few enemy aircraft would attack the island every night. American transports were never seriously threatened, and the Japanese fleet never joined the battle. Japanese troops began to commit suicide rather than risk being captured.

Col. Shoup noticed the shift in momentum. Despite his frustration over the miscommunications and delays, he was in good spirits. He sent a situation report to Gen. Smith at 1600 —with a famous last line:

Casualties: many. Percentage dead: unknown. Combat efficiency: We are winning.

At 1655, the 2/6 landed on Bairiki against light opposition. During the night, the 2/10 landed on the same island and began firing its howitzers. Rixey's fire direction center on Betio helped this process. The forward artillery observer, attached to Maj. Crowe's 2/8 on Red Beach One, adjusted the fire of the Bairiki guns he'd practiced on in New Zealand. Gen. Smith finally had artillery in place on Bairiki.

Meanwhile, the 1/6 were finally on the move. After a day of many false starts, the Marines prepared for their assault mission, which Gen. Smith had changed from the east end to Green Beach. When the *Feland* returned to within a reasonable range, the 1/6 Marines disembarked. They used the tactics developed with the Navy during the rehearsal on Efate. The men loaded onboard the Higgins boat's, which towed their rubber raft to the beach. The Marines embarked on board the rafts with up to ten troops per craft and began the 1,000-yard paddle toward Green Beach.

Major "Willie K." Jones, commander of the 1/6 Marines, later remarked that he did *not* feel like the "admiral of the condom fleet," as he helped paddle his raft shoreward. He noted that his battalion was spread out over the ocean from horizon to horizon. Maj. Jones was alarmed at the frequent appearance of anti-boat mines moored to the coral heads beneath the surface, endangering his 150 rubber rafts.

His rafts passed over the mines without incident. Jones also had two LVTs accompanying his ship to shore movement, each preloaded with rations, ammo, water, medical supplies, and spare radio equipment. While guided in by the rafts, one of the LVTs made it ashore, but the second drifted into a mine that blew the heavy vehicle ten feet in the air, killed most of the crew, and destroyed all of the supplies. It was a severe but not critical loss. The landing force suffered no other casualties coming ashore, thanks to Maj. Ryan's men. Jones' battalion was the first to land intact on Betio.

It was well after dark by the time Maj. Jones assumed his defensive positions behind Maj. Ryan's lines. The light tanks of Company B continued their attempt to come ashore on Green Beach. Because of the high surf and the distance between the reef, the beach hindered the landing effort. While a platoon of six tanks eventually reached the beach, the rest of the company moved its boats toward the pier and worked all night to get ashore onto Red Beach Two. The 3/6 Marines remained afloat in Higgins boats beyond the reef for an uncomfortable night.

That evening Col. Shoup turned to war correspondent Robert Sherrod and said:

We're winning, but the bastards have a lot of bullets left. I think we should clean it all up tomorrow.

After dark, Gen. Smith sent Col. Edson ashore to command all Betio and Bairiki forces. Col. Shoup had done a magnificent job, but it was now time for the senior colonel to take command. Edson had two artillery battalions and eight reinforced infantry battalions deployed on the two islands.

The 3/6 Marines were scheduled to land early on D+2. Virtually all combat and support elements of the 2nd Marine Division would now be deployed.

Col. Edson found Shoup's command post at 2030. He greeted the barrel-chested warrior still on his feet, haggard and grimy but full of fight. Col. Edson took command and allowed Col. Shoup to concentrate on his own reinforced combat team, and they began making plans for the next morning.

Years later, Gen. Julian Smith looked back on the pivotal day of November 21, 1943, and wrote:

We were losing until we won. Many things went wrong, and the Japanese inflicted severe casualties on us, but from this point on, the issue was no longer in doubt at Tarawa.

D+2 AT BETIO

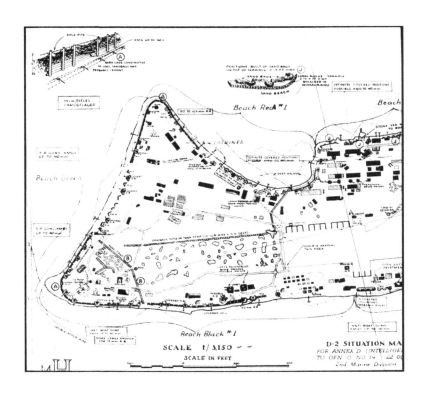

152

War correspondent Keith Wheeler from *the Chicago Daily News* sent this dispatch from Tarawa on D+2:

It looks like the Marines are winning on this blood-soaked, bomb-hammered, stinking little island.

Col. Edson's plan of attack on D+2 was to have the 1/6 Marines attack eastward along south beach and link up with the 1/2 and 2/2. He issued his attack orders at 0400 and attached the 1/8 to the 2nd Division Marines. They were to attack at daylight to the west along north beach and eliminate all Japanese resistance pockets between Red Beach One and Two. After that, the 1/8 would continue the attack east.

Edson arranged for air support and naval gunfire to strike the eastern end of the island at twenty-minute intervals throughout the morning. The 3/6 Marines were still embarked at the line of departure and would await Col. Shoup's call on Green Beach.

The key to the success of this plan was an eastward attack by fresh troops from Maj. Jones' landing team. Col. Edson could not raise the 1/6 on any radio net and sent his assistant division operations officer, Maj. Tompkins, to deliver the attack order in person to Jones. Maj. Tompkins' odyssey from the command post to Green Beach took over three hours. He was almost shot, several times, by Japanese snipers and nervous American sentries. The radio net started to work again just before Tompkins reached the 1/6 Marines. Maj. Jones later wrote he never told Tompkins he already had the attack order when the exhausted messenger arrived.

Maj. Hays promptly launched his attack at 0700 on Red Beach Two. He attacked westward on a three company front. His engineers used Bangalore torpedoes and satchel charges to neutralize many inland Japanese positions. But the strongpoints along the re-entrant were a deadly and veritable hornet's nest. Light Marine tanks made courageous frontal attacks against the Japanese fortifications. The tanks fired their 37mm guns point-blank at the Japanese fortifications, but were inadequate for the task. One tank was destroyed because of enemy fire, and the other two withdrew. Maj. Hays called for a section of 75mm half-tracks. One half-track was lost instantly, but the others used their more massive guns to considerable advantage.

The left flank and center companies curved around behind the main Japanese strongpoints, cutting the enemy off from the rest of the island. Along the beach, the progress was measured in yards. A small Japanese party tried a sortie from the strong points against the Marine lines. Now the Marines were finally given actual targets in the open—they cut the Japanese down in short order.

Maj. Jones made his final preparations for the assault to the east on Green Beach, with the 1/6 Marines. He had access to several light tanks available from the platoon that came ashore the prior evening. Maj. Jones preferred the medium tanks' effectiveness and borrowed two medium battle-scarred Sherman's from Ryan for the assault. Maj. Jones ordered the tanks to range no further than fifty yards ahead of his lead company. He personally kept in radio contact with the tank commander. Jones assigned a platoon of .30-caliber water-cooled machine guns to each rifle company and attached combat engineers with flamethrowers and demolition squads. Due to the nature of the terrain and the necessity for giving Maj. Hays' battalion a wide berth, Jones constrained his attack to a zone of only one-hundred yards wide. In his words:

This was one of the most unusual tactics I'd ever heard of. As I moved to the east on one side of the airfield, Larry Hays moved to the west of me, exactly opposite.

Maj. Jones' plan was well executed. He had the advantage of a fresh tactical unit in place with integrated supporting arms. The 1/6 Marine landing team made rapid progress along the south coast, killing over two hundred Japanese defenders. American casualties were light at this point, and he reached the thin lines held by the 2/2 and the 1/2 in less than three hours.

Col. Shoup called Maj. Jones to his command post at 1100 to brief him on the afternoon plan of action. Major Jones' XO, Major Francis Beamer, was to take and replace the lead rifle company. Enemy resistance had stiffened, and the company commander had just been shot and killed by a sniper. The oppressive heat was taking its toll on the Marines. While Beamer made superhuman efforts to get more salt tablets and water for his men, several of his troops had fallen out and become victims of heatstroke. First Sergeant Lewis Michelony later wrote:

Tarawa's sands were as white as snow and as hot as red white ashes from a heated furnace.

On Green Beach, only 800 yards behind the 1/6 Marines, the landing team of the 3/6 Marines streamed to shore. While the landing took several hours to execute, it was uncontested. Not until 1100 did Maj. Jones' lead elements link up with the 2nd Marines before the 3/6 were fully established onshore.

The 8th Marines attack order was the same as the

previous day: attack Japanese strong points to the east. These obstacles were just as difficult on D+2. Three of the Japanese fortifications were especially formidable:

1. A steel pillbox near the contested pier
2. A large bombproof shelter further inland
3. A coconut log emplacement with multiple machine guns

All three obstacles had been designed by the master engineer, Adm. Saichiro. These strongpoints, mutually supported by fire and observation, had effectively contained the combined Marine forces of the 3/8 and the 2/8 since the assault on D-Day.

Maj. Crowe reorganized his tired forces into another assault. The former marksmanship instructor got cans of lubricating oil out and made his troops field strip and clean their M1s before the attack. Crowe placed his Battalion XO, Major William Chamberlin, in the center of the three attacking. Chamberlin was a former college economics professor and was no less dynamic than his red mustached commander. Still nursing a painful wound in his shoulder received at D-Day, Chamberlin was a major player in the repetitive assaults against the three Japanese strong points. 1stSgt. Michelony later wrote about Chamberlin:

He was a wild man, a guy anybody would be willing to follow.

Chamberlin took his mortar crew and scored a direct hit on top of the coconut log emplacement at 0930. He penetrated the bunker and detonated the ammunition stocks. It was a stroke of great fortune for the Marines. At the same time, the medium tank *Colorado* penetrated the steel pillbox with its 75mm guns. Now, two of the three emplacements were overrun.

The massive bombproof shelter was still lethal. Flanking attacks were getting shot to pieces before they could gather any momentum. The solution was to get to the top of the sand-covered mound and drop thermite grenades or explosives down the air vents to force the Japanese outside. This formidable task went to Maj. Chamberlin, Lt. Alexander Bonnyman, and a squad of combat engineers.

Machine gunners and riflemen opened up a sheet of fire against the strongpoint's firing ports. Bonnyman led a small band and raced across the sands up the steep slope. The Japanese knew they were in mortal danger. Dozens of them poured out of the rear entrance, attacking the Marines on top. A Marine stepped forward and emptied his flamethrower into the onrushing Japanese—then charged them with an M1 carbine. The Marine was shot dead and his body rolled down the slope. But other Marines were inspired to overcome the Japanese counterattack.

The remaining combat engineers rushed to place explosives against the rear entrances. Hundreds of demoralized Japanese broke out in panic and fled eastward; the Marines shot them to pieces. The tank crew fired one "dream shot" canister round. It killed at least twenty Japanese.

Lt. Bonnyman's bravery resulted in a posthumous Medal of Honor. The third to be awarded to the Marines on Betio. His single-handed sacrifice almost ended the stalemate on Red Beach Three. There's no coincidence that two of these highest awards were received by combat engineers. The bravery and courage under fire represented hundreds of other engineers on only a slightly less spectacular basis. Almost an entire third of the combat engineers who landed in support of the 2/8 ended up as casualties. According to

Second Lieutenant Beryl W. Rentel, the surviving combat engineers used:

Eight cases of TNT, eight cases of gelatin dynamite, and two 54-pound blocks of TNT to destroy Japanese fortifications. The engineers used an entire case of dynamite and both large blocks of TNT to destroy the large bombproof shelter alone.

STRONG RESISTANCE

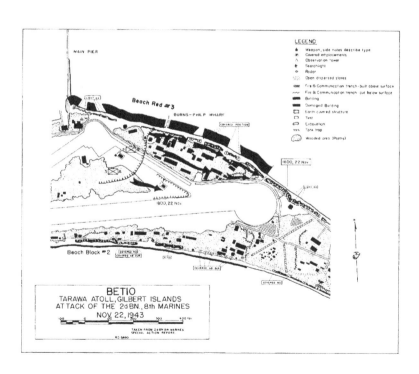

LEGEND

Weapon, side notes describe type
Covered emplacements
Observation tower
Searchlight
Radar
Open dispersed stores
Fire & Communication trench - built above surface
Fire & Communication trench - cut below surface
Building
Damaged Building
Earth covered structure
Tent
Excavation
Tank trap
Wooded area (Palms)

MAIN PIER

Beach Red #3

BURNS - PHILP WHARF

COVERED POSITION

1600, 22 Nov

1800, 22 Nov

Beach Block #2

COVERED MG

COVERED 48 GUN

COVERED 48 GUN

COVERED MG

BETIO
TARAWA ATOLL, GILBERT ISLANDS
ATTACK OF THE 2d BN., 8th MARINES
NOV. 22, 1943

TAKEN FROM 2d BN 8th MARINES
SPECIAL ACTION REPORT.

RD 5490

DURING THE CHAOTIC, murderous fighting in the 8th Marines'
zone, Adm. Shibasaki was killed in his blockhouse. The

DANIEL WRINN

unyielding Japanese commander's failure to provide any backup communications to the above-ground wires, which were destroyed during the preliminary D-Day bombardment, kept him from influencing the battle. The Imperial Japanese archives showed that Shibasaki transmitted one last message to Tokyo early in the morning on D+2:

Our weapons have been destroyed. From now on, everyone is attempting the final charge. May Japan exist for 10,000 years.

Gen. Julian Smith arrived on Green Beach just before noon. Smith conferred with Maj. Ryan and observed the deployment of the 3/6 Marines inland. Gen. Smith realized he was far removed from the main action toward the center of the island. He returned to his landing craft and ordered the coxswain to make for the pier. It was here that the commanding general received his rude welcome to Betio.

Maj. Hays' 1/8 Marines were besieging the Japanese strongpoints at the re-entrant. But the Japanese defenders still had control over the approaches to Red Beaches One and Two. The defenders' well-aimed machine gun fire disabled Smith's boat and killed his coxswain. The other occupants of his group leaped over the gunwale and into the water. Maj. Tompkins, the right man in the right place, waded through Japanese fire for a half-mile to find the general another LVT. This LVT drew fire and wounded the coxswain, further alarming the remaining occupants. Gen. Smith did not reach Col. Edson and Shoup's combined command post until 1400.

In the meantime, Col. Edson had assembled his commanders and issued orders to continue the attack to the east that afternoon. The 1/6 Marines would continue along the narrowing south coast, supported by the howitzers and all available tanks from the 1/10. Col. Hall would lead two battalions of the 8th Marines and continue advancing along the north coast. Air support and naval gunfire would blast the areas for two hours in advance.

Col. Hall spoke up about his exhausted and decimated Marine landing teams. They'd been in direct contact and ashore since D-Day morning. He told Edson the two landing teams had enough strength for only one more assault, and then they must get relieved.

Col. Edson promised to exchange the exhausted 2/8 Marines with the fresh 2/6 Marines on Bairiki at the first opportunity after this assault.

The 1/6 Marines started their attack at 1330. They ran into heavy opposition. They took deadly fire from heavy Japanese weapons mounted in turret type emplacements near the south beach. While this took ninety minutes to overcome, the light tanks were brave but ineffective. It took sustained 75mm fire, from two Sherman medium tanks, to neutralize the Japanese emplacements. Resistance was fierce throughout the zone, and the 1/6 Marines' casualties mounted. They'd taken eight-hundred-yards of enemy territory quickly in the morning, but by the long afternoon had attained half that distance.

The 8th Marines, after having destroyed their three bunker nemesis, made excellent progress at first, but then ran out of steam after they passed the eastern end of the airfield. Col. Shoup was right in his estimation that the Japanese defenders, while leaderless, still had plenty of bullets and fight left.

Maj. Crowe reorganized his leading elements into defensive positions for the night. He placed one company north of the airfield. The end of the airstrip was covered by fire, but unmanned.

On nearby Bairiki Island, the 2/10 Marines fired artillery

missions to support Maj. Crowe. Company B of the 2nd Medical Battalion established a field hospital, handling the overflow of casualties. The 2/6 Marines, eager to get into the fight, waited in vain for boats to move them onto Green Beach. Landing craft were mostly unavailable. They were crammed with miscellaneous supplies as the transports and cargo ships continued a general unloading—regardless of the troops' needs ashore. Navy Seabees on Betio were already repairing the airstrip with bulldozers, under enemy fire. Occasionally, Marines would call in for help from the Seabees to seal up a bothersome bunker. A bulldozer would arrive and do the job nicely.

Shore party Marines and Navy beachmasters on the pier kept the supplies coming in and the wounded going out. Col. Edson requested a working party at 1552 to clear bodies from around the pier that hindered shore party operations. Later that afternoon the first Jeep got ashore. A wild ride along the pier with every remaining Japanese sniper trying to shoot the driver. War correspondent Sherrod commented:

If a sign of certain victory was needed, this is it. The jeeps have arrived.

One of Col. Hall's Navajo Indian code-talkers had been mistaken for a Japanese and was shot. This was because of the strain of the prolonged battle. A derelict, blackened LVT drifted onshore filled with dead Marines. At the bottom of the pile was one Marine who was still alive. Still breathing, after two-and-a-half days of an unrelenting hell. He looked up and gasped, "Water. Pour some water on my face, will you?"

Shoup, Edson, and Smith were near exhaustion. While the third day on Betio had been a day of spectacular gains, progress was excruciatingly slow. And the end was not in sight.

Gen. Smith sent this report to Gen. Hermle, who had taken his place on the *Maryland*:

Situation not favorable for rapid cleanup on Betio. Heavy casualties among officers make leadership difficult. Still strong resistance. Many emplacements intact on eastern end of the island. Japanese strong points westward of our front lines within our position have not been reduced. Progress costly and slow. Complete occupation will take at least five days more. Air and naval bombardment a great help but does not take out emplacements.

Gen. Smith took command of operations at 1930. He had seven thousand Marines onshore fighting against one thousand Japanese defenders. Aerial photographs showed many defensive positions were still intact on Betio's eastern tail. Smith believed he would need the entire 6th Marines to complete the job. At 2100 the 6th Marines landed. Smith called a meeting to assign orders for D+3.

The 3/6 Marines would pass through the lines of Maj. Jones' 1/6 Marines to have a fresh Battalion lead the eastward assault. The 2/6 Marines would land on Green Beach and move east to support the 3/6. All available tanks would be assigned to the 3/6. Col. Shoup's 2nd Marines, with the 1/8 still attached, would continue to assault the Japanese re-entrant strongpoints. The remaining 8th Marines would be shuttled to Bairiki. The 4/10 would land its heavy 105mm guns on Green Beach to increase the howitzer battalions' firepower that was already in action.

Imperial Japanese soldiers began vicious counterattacks during the nights of D+2 and D+3. Maj. Jones believed his exposed forces would be the target for any *Banzai* attacks and took his precautions. He gathered his artillery forward observers and naval fire control spotters. Jones arranged for field artillery support starting from seventy-five yards from his front lines to 500 yards out, where naval gunfire would take over. Maj. Jones put Company A to the left of the airstrip and Company B on the right along the south shore; while he worried about the 150-yard gap across the runway to Company C, he realized there was no solution. Jones used a tank to bring up stockpiles of small arms ammunition, grenades, and water to be kept fifty yards behind the lines.

At 1930, the first Japanese counterattack began. Fifty Japanese soldiers snuck past Maj. Jones' outposts through thick vegetation and penetrated the border between the two companies south of the airstrip. Maj. Jones' reserve force was composed of his headquarters' cooks, bakers, and admin people. They contained the penetration and killed many Japanese in the two hours of close-in fighting. Direct and intense fire from the howitzers of the 1/10 and 2/10 stopped the Japanese from reinforcing their penetration. By 2130, the lines were stabilized, and Maj. Jones placed a company one hundred yards to the rear of his lines. All he had left was a composite force of forty Marines.

At 2300, the Japanese attacked Jones' lines again. They made a loud disturbance across from Company A's lines. Clinking canteens against their helmets, taunting Marines and screaming *Banzai*, while a second force attacked Company B in a silent rush. The Marines repelled this attack but used their machine guns, revealing their positions. Maj. Jones requested a full company from the 3/6 to reinforce the 2nd Marines to the rear of the fighting.

The third attack came at 0300. The Japanese moved multiple 7.7mm machine guns into nearby wrecked trucks and opened fire on Marine weapons positions. Maj. Jones called for star shell illumination from the destroyers in the lagoon. A

Marine sergeant crawled forward against this oncoming fire to lob grenades into the improvised machine-gun nests. This did the job and silenced the battlefield once again.

Three hundred Japanese launched a frenzied attack at 0400 against the same two Marine companies. The Marines repulsed them with every available weapon. Japanese soldiers were caught in a murderous crossfire from the 10th Marine howitzers. Two destroyers in the lagoon, *Sigsbee* and *Schroeder,* opened up on the Japanese flanks. Waves of screaming attackers took vicious casualties but kept coming. Groups of men locked together in bloodied hand-to-hand combat. PFC Jack Stambaugh of Company B killed three Japanese soldiers with his bayonet before an officer beheaded him with a samurai sword. Another Marine jumped in and knocked out the Japanese officer with his rifle butt. The acting commander of Company B, First Lieutenant Norman Thomas, reached Major Jones on the field phone and said:

We're killing them as fast as they come at us, but we can't hold out much longer. We need reinforcements.

Maj. Jones replied:

We haven't got them. You've got to hold.

The Marines lost 42 dead and 114 wounded in the wild fighting—but they held. In less than an hour, it was all over. The supporting arms never stopped shooting down the Japanese, either attacking or retreating. Both destroyers emptied their magazines of 5-inch shells. The 1/10 Marines fired over 1,400 rounds that night. As dawn broke, Marines counted over 200 dead Japanese within fifty yards of their lines. An additional 130 bodies laid beyond that range, badly mangled by naval and artillery gunfire. Other bodies laid scattered throughout the Marine lines. Maj. Jones had to blink back his tears of pride and grief as he walked his lines. One of his Marines grabbed his arm and said:

They told us we had to hold, and by God, we did.

COMPLETING THE TASK

JAPANESE COUNTERATTACKS during the nights of November 22 and 23 broke the back of their defense. If they'd remained in their bunkers until the bitter end, the enemy could have taken a higher toll of Marine lives. Rather than facing an inevitable defeat, over 600 Japanese soldiers chose to die by taking an offensive night action.

After the bloody counterattacks during the night, the 2nd Marine Division still had over five more hours of tough fighting on Betio before the island could be conquered. Later in the morning Gen. Smith sent this report to Adm. Hill on the *Maryland*:

Enemy counterattack was defeated decisively. Last night destroyed bulk of hostile resistance. Expect complete annihilation of all enemy on Betio this date. Recommend you and staff come ashore to get information on type of hostile resistance which will be encountered in future operations.

After a preliminary bombardment, the fresh troops of the

3/6 Marines weaved through Maj. Jones' lines and began their attack to the east. The Marine assault tactics were now well refined. The 3/6 Marines made rapid progress, led by tanks and combat engineers with flamethrowers and high explosives. Only one well-armed bunker, along the north shore, provided any substantial opposition.

The 3/6 Marines took advantage of the heavy brush along the south shore and bypassed the obstacle. They left one rifle company to encircle and eventually overrun it. Momentum was with the Marines. The remaining Japanese troops seemed dispirited. By 1300, the 3/6 reached the eastern tip of Betio and inflicted over five hundred Japanese casualties at the loss of only thirty-four Marines.

Lieutenant Colonel MacLeod sent a report that summarized the Japanese defenders' collapse in the eastern zone that followed their counterattacks:

At no time was there any determined defensive. We used flamethrowers and could've used more. Medium tanks were excellent. Light tanks did not fire one shot.

The hardest fighting of the fourth day was on the border of Red Beach One and Two. Col. Shoup directed the combined forces of the 1/8 and 3/2 against the re-entrant strongpoint. The Japanese in these positions were the most disciplined and deadliest on the island. In these bunkers, Japanese anti-boat gunners had thoroughly disrupted over four different battalions' landings and almost killed Gen. Smith the day before. The seaward approaches to the strongpoints were littered with bloated bodies and destroyed LVTs.

Maj. Hays finally received his flamethrowers and began the attack with the 1/8 from the east, making steady—painstaking progress. Maj. Schoettel was eager to atone for what may have been perceived as a lackluster performance on D-Day. Schoettel attacked and pressed the assault with troops from the 3/2 from the west and south. Completing the circle, Col. Shoup ordered a platoon of infantry and two 75mm half-tracks out to the reef, keeping the enemy pinned down from the lagoon.

The exhausted Japanese defenders either fought to the end or committed *hara-kiri*. The 1/8 Marines had been attacking this fortified strongpoint ever since the bloodied landing on the morning of D+1. In only forty-eight hours, the 1/8 Marines fired over 55,000 rounds of .30-caliber rifle ammo. The real damage was done by the engineers' special weapons, and by direct fire from the 75mm half-tracks. After the Marines captured the largest concrete pillbox position near the beach, they could approach the remaining bunkers more safely. It was all over by 1300.

When the fighting was still underway, a Navy fighter plane landed on Betio's airstrip and weaved around the Seabee trucks. Marines rushed over to the aircraft to shake the pilot's hand.

At 1245, Adm. Hill and his staff came ashore. The senior naval officers were impressed by the great strength of the Japanese bunker system. They realized the need to reorganize bombardment strategies. Adm. Hill praised the Marines for making such a landing and called Betio a "little Gibraltar."

When Col. Shoup reported to Gen. Smith that the ultimate objectives had been seized, Smith shared the excellent news with Adm. Hill. Between them, they had worked together to achieve this victory. They drafted a message to Adm. Turner and Gen. Holland Smith announcing the end of organized resistance on Betio.

Working parties were organized to identify the dead. Many of the bodies were so severely shattered or burned that it was difficult to distinguish between friend and foe. The stench and decay of death was overwhelming. War correspondent Robert Sherrod wrote:

Betio would be more habitable if the Marines could leave for a few days, and the million buzzards swirling overhead could finish their work.

Chaplains accompanied burial teams equipped with bulldozers. Administrative staff worked diligently to prepare accurate casualty lists. Even more casualties were expected in mop-up operations over the surrounding islands including Apamama, also known as Abemama Atoll. A distressing report was issued that over one-hundred Marines were missing. The changing tides swept many bodies of the assault troops out to sea. One of the first pilots ashore reported seeing dozens of floating corpses miles away over the horizon.

The Japanese defenders were nearly annihilated in the battle. The Marines, supported by carrier aviation, naval gunfire, and Army Air Force units, killed 98% of the 4,836 enemy troops on Betio during the assault. Only seventeen Japanese soldiers were taken prisoner. The only Japanese officer captured in the fighting was Kiyoshi Ota. A thirty-year-old ensign in the *7th Sasebo Special Landing Force*, from Nagasaki. Ensign Ota recounted that the Japanese garrison had expected landings along the southwest sectors instead of the northern beaches. He also believed the reef would have protected the Japanese defenders during the low tide.

Before Gen. Julian Smith announced the Marines' victory at Betio, Gen. Ralph Smith, his Army counterpart, reported: "Makin Taken." In three days of hard fighting over on Butaritari Island, the Army had wiped out the Japanese garrison at the cost of 204 American casualties.

Many exhausted and grimy Marines on Betio had been awake since the night before the landing. Capt. Carl Hoffman later wrote in his memoirs:

There was no way to rest. There was virtually no way to eat. Most of it was close, hand-to-hand fighting, and survival for three and a half days. One of my men mixed me a canteen full of hot water, coffee, chocolate, sugar, he gave it to me and told me he thought I needed something. It was the best meal I'd ever had.

Marines were surrounded by the devastation on Betio after the fighting. Chaplain Willard walked along Red Beach One, now finally clear of enemy pillboxes, and scratched out a note to his wife:

I'm on Tarawa in the midst of the worst destruction I've ever seen. Walking along the shore, I counted seventy-six dead Marines staring up at me, half in and half out of the water. An LVT is jammed against the seawall barricade. Three waterlogged Marines lay dead beneath it. Four others are scattered nearby, and there is one hanging on a 2-foot high strand of barbed wire who doesn't even touch the coral flat at all. What I see in this god-awful place I am certain is one of the greatest works of ruin wrought by any man.

Japanese forces in the Gilbert Islands took a bloody toll from the Marine invasion force. Japanese submarines arrived in the area during D+2. The *I-175* sunk the carrier *Liscome Bay* with a torpedo as the sun rose on November 24 off of Makin. A horrific explosion—the flash was seen at Tarawa, over 90 miles away—the ship sank quickly, taking 644 souls with her to the bottom.

The Marines conducted a flag-raising ceremony later that same morning. There were few surviving palm trees to select as a flagpole. A field musician played the bugle calls, and Marines all over the island stood and saluted. Each reckoning the cost.

More good news came from the V Amphibious Corps Reconnaissance Company. They had landed on Apamama by rubber rafts from the submarine *Nautilus*. On the night of November 21, while the small Japanese garrison kept the scouts at bay, the *Nautilus* surfaced and fired its deck guns, killing many Japanese defenders—the rest committed *hara-kiri*. After the island was deemed secure, the 3/6 Marines took control of Apamama until other defense forces could arrive.

On November 24, amphibious transports entered the lagoon and loaded Marine combat teams 2 and 8. Many Marines believed going back to a ship, after the carnage of

Betio, was like going to heaven. Navy personnel were generous and kind. The Marines were treated to a full-scale turkey dinner served by Navy officers. Many Marines still suffered from post-combat trauma.

The 2nd and 8th Marines were on their way to Hawaii, while the 3/6 Marines were on their way to Apamama. The 2/6 Marines were beginning their long trek through the other islands of the Tarawa atoll. Under Maj. Jones, the 1/6 Marines were the last infantry unit on Betio. Their work was tedious and heartbreaking. They buried the dead, flushed out the last of the diehard snipers, and hosted visiting dignitaries.

Gen. Holland Smith, the V Amphibious Corps commander, flew to Betio on November 24. He spent an emotional afternoon viewing the death and destruction with Gen. Julian Smith. Gen. Holland Smith was shaken by what he'd seen and the Marines' sacrifices on the island. He concluded:

The sight of our dead Marines floating in the waters of the lagoon and lying along the blood-caked beaches is one I will never forget. Over the pitted, blasted island hung a miasma of coral dust and death, nauseating and horrifying.

The generals came upon one site that moved all of them to tears. A dead Marine leaned against a seawall, his arm upright from his body weight. Just beyond his upraised hand on top of the seawall was a blue-and-white flag. A beach marker to direct succeeding waves where to land. Gen. Holland Smith cleared his throat and said, "How can men like that ever be defeated?"

Company D of the 2nd Tank battalion was the designated scout company for Tarawa's 2nd Marine Division. Elements of these scouts had landed on the Buota and Eita Islands while the fighting raged on Betio. The scouts discovered a sizable Japanese force. On November 23, the 3/10 Marines landed on Eita. The battalion's howitzers were initially intended to increase support fire on Betio. When the island finally fell, the artillery turned their guns to support the 2/6 clearing out the rest of the islets in the Tarawa Atoll.

At 0500 on November 24, the 2/6 Marine landing team under Colonel Murray boarded boats from Betio and landed on Buota. Murray moved his Marines at a fierce pace, wading across the sandspits that joined the succeeding islands. Murray learned from friendly natives that a Japanese infantry force of 175 waited ahead on the larger island of Buariki. The lead elements of the 2/6 caught up with the enemy on November 26. After a sharp fire exchange in thick vegetation, Murray pulled his troops back. He positioned his forces for an all-out assault in the morning.

The November 27, Battle of Buariki was the last engagement in the Gilberts. It was no less deadly than the preceding encounter with the *Special Naval Landing Forces*. Col. Murray assaulted the Japanese defensive positions at dawn. He received supporting fire from Battery G before the lines became too intermingled in the melee.

The fighting was not unlike Guadalcanal: hand-to-hand brawling in the tangled underbrush. The Japanese did not have the elaborate defenses found on Betio. But the Imperial Naval soldiers took advantage of as much cover and concealment as they could. They made every shot count and fought to the death. All 175 of them were killed. Col. Murray's victory came at a high cost. 32 Marines killed and 60 more wounded. The next day, the Marines crossed to the last islet and found no more Japanese defenders. Gen. Julian Smith announced on November 28 that the remaining enemy forces on Tarawa had been wiped out.

Adm. Nimitz had arrived on Betio just before Gen. Julian

Smith's announcement. Nimitz noted that the primary Japanese defenses were still intact. He had his staff diagnose the exact construction methods the Japanese used. In less than a month, an identical set of pillboxes and bunkers were built on naval bombardment islands in the Hawaiian island chain.

Adm. Nimitz presented a few of the many to come combat awards to the 2nd Division Marines. The Presidential Unit Citation was awarded to the entire division. Col. Shoup received the Medal of Honor. Maj. Crowe and his XO, Maj. Chamberlin, received the Navy Cross, as well as LtCol. Amey, Maj. Ryan, and Cpl. Spillane--the LVT crew chief and St. Louis Cardinals prospect, who caught the Japanese hand grenades in midair on D-Day before his luck ran out.

While some senior officers were jealous of Col. Shoup's Medal of Honor, Gen. Julian Smith knew whose strong shoulders carried the critical first thirty-six hours of the assault. Col. Shoup recorded in his combat notebook:

With God and the Navy in support of the 2nd Marine Division, there was never any doubt that we would take Betio. For several hours, however, there was a considerable haggling over the exact price we would pay for it.

SIGNIFICANCE OF TARAWA

THE HIGH COST of the battle for Tarawa was twofold: the Marine casualties in the assault, followed by the nation's despair and shock after hearing the battle reports. At first, the gains seemed small. The "stinking little island" of Betio was eight thousand miles away from Tokyo. But the practical lessons learned in the complexity of amphibious assault outweighed the initial public outrage.

Casualty figures for the 2nd Marine Division and Operation Galvanic were 3,407. There were 1,027 dead Marines and sailors. An additional 88 Marines were missing and presumed dead, and 2,292 Marines and sailors wounded. Guadalcanal's campaign cost a similar number of Marine casualties—but spread over six months.

Tarawa losses happened in 76 hours. The killed to wounded ratio at Tarawa was excessive and reflected the savagery of the fighting. Overall, the casualties among the Marines engaged in the fight was around 19%. A steep but *acceptable* price. Many battalions suffered much higher losses. The 2nd Amphibian Tractor Battalion lost half of their men. This battalion also lost 35 of the 125 LVTs on Betio.

Headlines of "The Bloody Beaches of Tarawa" alarmed the American public. This was partially the Marines' own doing. Many combat correspondents were invited along for Operation Galvanic. They had shared the worst of what Betio had to offer in the first thirty-six hours. They only reported what they had observed. Marine Sgt. James Lucas, whose account of the fighting received front-page coverage in both *The New York Times* and *The Washington Post* on December 4, 1943, read:

Grim Tarawa Defense a Surprise, Eyewitness of Battle Reveals; Marines Went in Chuckling, To Find Swift Death Instead of Easy Conquest.

Remarks made by senior Marines involved in Operation Galvanic to the media did little to help soothe public concerns. Gen. Holland Smith likened the assault on D-Day to Pickett's charge at Gettysburg. Col. Edson said the assault force "paid the stiffest price in human life per square yard" at Tarawa than any other engagement in the Marine Corps' history. War correspondent Robert Sherrod wrote of seeing one-hundred Marines gunned down in the water in five minutes on D+1. It did not help when the Marine Corps headquarters waited an additional ten days after the battle to release the casualty list.

The atmospheres at Pearl Harbor and Washington were tense during this period. General Douglas MacArthur was still bitter that the 2nd Marine Division had been taken from his Southwest Pacific Command. He wrote to the Secretary of War and complained that "these frontal attacks by the Navy, like Tarawa, were unnecessary and a tragic massacre of American lives."

American mothers wrote letters by the hundreds, one accusing Adm. Nimitz of "murdering her son."

Frank Knox, the secretary of the Navy, called a press conference in which he blamed a "sudden shift in the wind" for exposing the reef and preventing reinforcements from landing. Congress began a special investigation. Fortunately, the Marines had General Vandegrift in Washington as the newly appointed 18th Commandant. Vandegrift, a highly decorated and widely respected veteran of Guadalcanal, reassured Congress and pointed out that "Tarawa was an assault from beginning to end."

The casualty reports were less extraordinary than the American public expected. In an editorial by *The New York Times* on December 27, 1943, the paper complemented the Marines for overcoming Tarawa's sophisticated defenses and zealous garrisons. The editorial warned that any future assaults, in the Marshall Islands, could be even deadlier:

We must steel ourselves now to pay that price.

After the war, the controversy continued when Gen. Holland Smith publicly claimed that Tarawa was a mistake. Adm. Nimitz replied by saying that Tarawa's capture knocked down the front door to the Japanese defenses in the Central Pacific.

Nimitz launched the Marshalls Campaign only ten weeks after the seizure of Tarawa. The photo-reconnaissance and attack aircraft from the captured airfields at Apamama and Betio proved vital.

The battle for Tarawa's capture would become the textbook on amphibious assault to guide and influence all subsequent landings in the Central Pacific. Nimitz believed that the prompt and selfless analysis immediately following Tarawa were of great value. He wrote:

From analytical reports of the commanders and from their critical evaluations of what went wrong, of what needed improvement, and of what techniques and equipment proved out in combat, came a tremendous outpouring of lessons learned.

Many senior officers later agreed that the conversion of the logistical LVTs to assault craft made the difference between victory and defeat on Betio. A further consensus was that the LVT-1s and LVT-2s used in the operation were only marginal against the heavily defensive fire. The LVT-1s (Alligators) needed heavier armament, more powerful engines, auxiliary bilge pumps, self-sealing gas tanks, and wooden plugs the size of 13mm bullets. More importantly, there needed to be more LVTs, at least 300 per division. Col. Shoup wanted to keep the use of LVTs as reef-crossing assault vehicles a secret, but there were too many reporters on the scene.

Naval gunfire got mixed reviews. Marines were enthusiastic about the destroyers' responses in the lagoon but critical about the preliminary bombardment's extent and accuracy—especially when it was ended so prematurely on D-Day. Maj. Ryan later wrote that the significant shortcomings in Operation Galvanic were:

Overestimating the damage that could be inflicted on a heavily defended position by an intense but limited naval bombardment, and by not sending in its assault forces soon enough after the shelling.

Maj. Schoettel later wrote that of the pounding his battalion received from emplacements within the seawall, he'd have recommended a direct fire against the beach by 40mm guns from close-in destroyers. The hasty saturation fires, considered adequate by planners because of strategic surprise, proved virtually useless. Any amphibious assaults against fortified atolls would need sustained, aimed, and deliberate fire.

No one could question the bravery of the aviators who supported the assault on Betio. But many questioned whether they were trained and armed adequately for such a difficult target. The need for closer integration of all supporting arms was clear.

Communications throughout the assault on Betio were terrible. Only the resourcefulness of a few radio operators and the bravery of individual runners kept the assault coherent. The Marines needed waterproof radios. The Navy needed a dedicated amphibious command ship, not on board a major combatant whose massive guns knocked out the radio nets with each salvo. These command ships, the AGC's, would appear later during the Marshalls Campaign.

Other amphibious revisions to the doctrine were immediately enacted. The priority of unloading supplies would become the tactical commander's call onshore, not the amphibious task force commander. Betio showed the critical need for underwater swimmers to stealthily assess and report the surf, beach, and reef conditions to the task force before the landing. This concept was first envisioned by amphibious warfare prophet Major Earl "Pete" Ellis in the 1920s, and quickly came to fruition. Adm. Turner created a fledgling UDT (Underwater Demolition Team) for the Marshall Islands assault.

The Marines also learned that the new medium tanks would become valuable assets with proper combined arms training. Future tank training would now emphasize integrated tank, engineer, infantry, and artillery operations. Tank and infantry communications would need immediate improvement. Most casualties among tank commanders on Betio resulted from individuals needing to dismount their vehicles to speak with the infantry in the open.

Backpack flamethrowers won universal approval from the Marines on Betio. Each commander recommended increases in range, quantity, and mobility for these assault weapons. Suggestions were that larger versions should be mounted on LVTs and tanks, predicting the appearance of "Zippo Tanks" in later Pacific campaigns.

Gen. Julian Smith summed up the lessons he learned at Tarawa with this comment:

We made fewer mistakes than the Japs did.

Military historian Philip A. Crowl wrote in his assessment of the battle for Tarawa:

The capture of Tarawa despite all defects in execution, conclusively demonstrated that the American amphibious doctrine was valid, that even the strongest island fortress could be seized.

Future landings in the Marshall Islands would use this doctrine to achieve objectives against similar targets with fewer casualties and in less time. The benefits of Operation Galvanic quickly outweighed the steep initial costs. In time, Tarawa became a symbol of sacrifice and courage for Marine raiders and Japanese defenders alike.

Ten years after the battle, Gen. Julian Smith saluted the heroism of the Japanese who chose to die almost to the last man. He then turned to his beloved 2nd Marine Division shipmates in Task Force 53 at Betio:

For the officers and men, Marines and sailors, who crossed that reef, either as assault troops, or carrying supplies, or evacuating wounded, I can only say that I shall forever think of them with the feeling of the greatest respect and reverence.

TARAWA TODAY

DECADES AFTER WORLD WAR II, Tarawa remains mostly unchanged. Visiting Betio Island, you can still see wrecked LVTs and American tanks along the beaches as well as ruined Japanese pillboxes and gun emplacements. The imposing concrete bunkers created by Adm. Shibasaki still stand, as impervious to time as they were to the naval guns of Task Force 53. At the turn of the century, island natives found a buried LVT containing skeletons of its Marine crew inside— one Marine still wearing his dog tags.

In 1968, Gen. David Shoup was recalled from retirement to active duty for nine days to dedicate a large monument on Betio. He commemorated the twenty-fifth anniversary of the famous fight and later told *The National Observer*:

My first reaction was that Betio Island had shrunk a great deal. It seems smaller now in peace than in war.

While Shoup toured the ruined fortifications, he recalled the desperate, savage fighting. He pondered why the two nations spent so much for so little. In seventy-six hours of fighting, nearly 6,000 Americans and Japanese died on the tiny island.

In the late 1980s, the American Memorial had fallen into disrepair. It was in danger of being dismantled for a cold storage plant to be used by Japanese fishermen. The 2nd Marine Division Association and Long Beach journalist, Tom Hennessey, began a lengthy campaign to raise enough funds to get a new, more stable monument. They brought a 9-ton block of Georgia granite with the inscription "To our fellow Marines, who gave their all." They dedicated this Memorial on November 20, 1988.

Betio is now part of the Republic of Kiribati. Tourist facilities have been developed to accommodate the large number of veterans who return every year. In author James Ullman's opinion, the small island still resembles what it probably looked like on D-Day almost 78 years ago. Ullman visited Tarawa several years ago and wrote a fitting eulogy:

A familiar irony that old battlefields are often the quietest and gentlest of places. It has been true of Gettysburg, Cannae, Austerlitz, Verdun—and is true of Tarawa.

MAJOR GENERAL JULIAN C. SMITH

THE PINNACLE of Gen. Smith's life and career was the epic
battle on Tarawa. At the time of Operation Galvanic, Smith

was fifty-eight years old and had been a Marine Corps officer for thirty-four years. He was born in Elkton, Maryland, and was a graduate of the University of Delaware.

He'd served overseas in the expeditionary tours of Nicaragua, Panama, Mexico, Haiti, and Santo Domingo. A Naval War College graduate in 1917, he spent WWI in Quantico, Virginia, with many other frustrated Marine officers.

Smith was a rifle team coach and a distinguished marksman. He had limited experience in the FMF (Fleet Marine Force). He took command of the 5th Marines in 1938 and was ordered to the 2nd Marine Division in May 1943.

Gen. Smith earned the respect of his contemporaries. While modest and humble, he had a fighting heart. Col. Ray Murray described him as a "fine old gentleman of high moral fiber. You'd fight for him."

Smith knew what to anticipate from the neap tides at Betio. In his memoirs, he wrote:

I'm an old railbird shooter up on the marshes of the Chesapeake Bay. You push over the marshes at high tide, and when you have a neap tide, you can't get over the marshes.

Gen. Smith was awarded the Navy Cross for his heroic acts in Nicaragua and the Distinguished Service Medal for his actions on Tarawa. While the balance of his career was unremarkable, he retired in 1946 as a lieutenant general and died at the age of 90 in 1975. He valued his experiences on Tarawa. In one of his last letters, he wrote:

It will always be a source of supreme satisfaction and pride to be able to say I was with the 2nd Marine Division at Tarawa.

COLONEL DAVID M. SHOUP

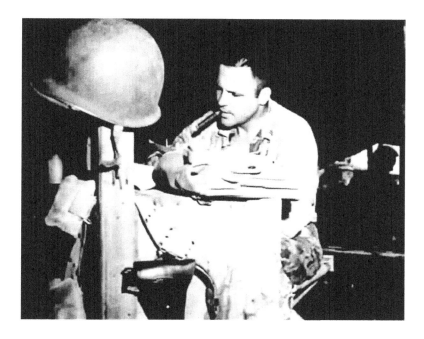

DAVID SHOUP CARRIED a field notebook during the battle of Tarawa. This passage gives us a glimpse into his enigmatic personality:

If you are qualified, fate has a way of getting you to the right place at the right time—tho' sometimes it appears to be a long, long wait.

A farm boy from Battle Ground, Indiana, the combination of time and place benefited Shoup on two momentous occasions: at Tarawa 1943, and as Pres. Eisenhower's selection to make him the 22nd Marine Corps Commandant in 1959.

Col. Shoup had been a Marine officer since 1926 and was thirty-eight years old during the battle of Tarawa. Unlike his colorful contemporaries, Shoup had limited experience as a commander and only the briefest exposure to combat. When Tarawa came, Shoup was a junior colonel in the 2nd Marine Division. He commanded eight battalion landing teams during some of the most savage fighting of World War II.

War correspondent Robert Sherrod later wrote of his impressions of Col. Shoup en route to Betio:

This Col. Shoup was an interesting character. A squat, red-faced man with a bull neck. He was a hard-boiled, profane shouter of orders. He carried the biggest burden on Tarawa.

Shoup was revered by his contemporaries as a "Marine's Marine." Sergeant Edward Doughman served with Shoup in China and on Tarawa. He described him as "the brainiest, nerviest, best soldiering Marine I ever met." Shoup had a reputation for being the most formidable poker player in the entire division because of his eyes that looked like "two burnt holes in a blanket."

Col. Shoup's Medal of Honor citation reflects his strength of character:

> *Upon arrival at the shore, he assumed command of all landed troops and worked with the rest under constant withering enemy fire. During the next two days, he conducted smashing attacks against incredibly strong and fanatically defended Japanese positions despite heavy casualties and innumerable obstacles.*

Shoup was a philosophical man. In his 1943 field notebook, he gave us some of his introspection:

> *I realize I am but a bit chaff from the threshings of life blown into the pages of history by the unknown winds of chance.*

David Shoup lived to the age of 78, dying on January 13, 1983. He was buried at Arlington National Cemetery.

1stSgt. Lewis J. Michelony Jr.

INCIDENT ON D+3

THE LAST DAY of fighting on Betio Island cost 1stSgt. Lewis Michelony his sense of smell. Michelony was a combat veteran of Guadalcanal, a 1/6 Marines member, and a former Atlantic Fleet boxing champion. Later in the Pacific War, he received two Silver Stars for conspicuous bravery. But on D+3, he nearly died.

Michelony was with two other Marines on a routine patrol of the area east of Green Beach. They looked for positions to assign the battalion mortar platoon. Infantry companies had cleared the area the previous morning. Other Marines had passed through the complex of seemingly empty Japanese bunkers without incident. The clearing was littered with Japanese bodies and abandoned enemy equipment. The three Marines threw grenades into the first bunker and encountered no response. All was quiet.

Then—out of nowhere—all hell broke loose. The front bunker opened fire with a machine gun, grenades hailed. In an instant, one Marine died; the second escaped, leaving 1stSgt. Michelony face down in the sand. Michelony dove into the nearest bunker, tumbled through a rear entrance, and landed into what he thought was a pool of water. The dim light of the bunker showed it was a combination of urine, blood, and water. It was a mixture from the dead Japanese bodies and from some live ones. He spat out the vile liquid in his mouth and realized there were still live Japanese among the dead and decaying. The taste, smell, and fear he experienced inside that bunker nearly overpowered him. In his own words:

Somehow I managed to get out. To this day, I don't know how. I crawled out of that cesspool, dripping wet. The sun-dried my utilities as though they had been heavily starched. But they still stank. For months after, I could still taste, smell, and visualize that scene.

Fifty years later, a retired Sergeant Major Michelony still had no sense of smell.

JAPANESE SPECIAL NAVAL LANDING FORCES

THE FIRST LARGE-SCALE encounter between the US Marines and the Japanese *Special Naval Landing Forces* was at Tarawa. Division staff had warned that the "naval units of this type were more highly trained and had a more remarkable tenacity and fighting spirit than the average Japanese army unit." But even the Marines were surprised at the ferocity of the defenders on Betio.

The Japanese Imperial Marines earned the respect of their US Marine Corps counterparts for their discipline, marksmanship, and proficiency with heavy weapons. The SNLF excelled in small unit leadership, bravery, and a willingness to die to the last man. Maj. Jones, who commanded the 1/6 Marines, had engaged more of the enemy in hand-to-hand combat on Betio than any unit. He later wrote:

These Japs were pretty tough, and they were big, all six feet, the biggest Japs I ever saw. Their equipment was excellent, and there was plenty of surplus found, including large amounts of ammo.

In the early years of the war, the Japanese used their SNLF frequently. In 1941, a force of 5,000 landed on Guam, and another 450 were used to assault Wake Island. A small detachment of 113 were the first Japanese reinforcing unit to land on Guadalcanal, ten days after the American landing.

The *Special Naval Landing Forces* gave a fierce resistance to the 1st Marine Division landings on Tulagi early in the Guadalcanal Campaign. A typical unit comprised of three rifle companies, augmented by antiaircraft and anti-boat guns, coastal defense, field artillery units, and labor troops, and was commanded by a naval captain.

The Japanese defenders on Betio used 7.7mm light machine guns. They integrated these weapons into their fortified defense system of over 500 blockhouses, pillboxes, and other placements. Most Marines faced the Japanese M93 during their landings on the northern coast. It was a 13mm, anti-air, anti-boat heavy machine gun. On many seawall emplacements, these deadly weapons provided flanking fire along the boat obstacles and wire entanglements.

Adm. Shibasaki organized his resistance on Betio for "an overall decisive defense at the beach." His troops fought with great bravery and valor. After seventy-six hours of savage fighting, 4,690 men lay dead. Out of 146 prisoners taken, most were conscripted Korean laborers.

Only seventeen wounded Japanese soldiers surrendered.

THE SINGAPORE GUNS

THE WORLD MEDIA claimed that the four 8-inch naval guns used as coastal defense guns by the Japanese were captured from the British at the fall of Singapore.

British writer William Bartsch visited Tarawa in 1977. Writing in his magazine, *After the Battle*, Bartsch examined each of the four guns and discovered the markings indicating manufacture by Vickers, a British ordnance company. The Vickers company presented Bartsch with records that the four guns were part of a consignment of twelve 8-inch, quick-firing guns, sold in 1905 to the Japanese during their war with Russia.

Further investigation at the Imperial War Museum revealed that no 8-inch guns were captured by the Japanese at Singapore. Tarawa's guns came from an older and far more legitimate transaction with the British.

The 8-inch guns that fired the opening salvo in the Battle of Tarawa were not a factor in the contest. Earlier bombing raids probably damaged their fire control systems. Rapid counter-battery fire from American battleships took out their big guns in short order. Col. Shoup wrote that the 2nd Marine Division was fully aware of 8-inch guns on Betio as early as mid-August 1943.

In contrast, Shoup's division intelligence reports, updated nine days before the landing, discounted any other reports that the guns were 8 inches. They insisted that they were probably no more than 6-inch.

The fact remains that many Marine officers were unpleasantly surprised to experience significant caliber near-misses assaulting the amphibious task force on D-Day.

LVT-2 AMPHIBIAN TRACTORS

THE LVT-2, also known as the Water Buffalo, improved upon the initial amphibious vehicle, the LVT-1, also known as the Alligator. A redesigned suspension system, rubber-tired road wheels, and torsion springs guaranteed a smoother ride and improved stability. The power train was standardized with that of the M3A1 light tank. This gave the Water Buffalo greater power and more reliability than its predecessor. With "W"

shape treads, it had better propulsion on land and in the water. Unlike the Alligator, the Water Buffalo was armored, which caused it to weigh significantly more. The Water Buffalo carried 1,400 pounds less cargo than the original LVT-1, but it kept its cargo safe from incoming fire.

In June 1942, the Water Buffalo entered production but did not see combat until Tarawa in November 1943. Marines used a combination of LVT-1s and LVT-2s in the Betio assault. Fifty LVTs used at Tarawa were modified in Samoa just before the battle. They installed 3/8 inch boiler plates around the cab for greater protection against shell fragments and small arms fire. Despite losing thirty vehicles to enemy fire at Tarawa, the improved armor was promising and led to the innovation of further armored LVTs.

The LVT-2(A), Buffalo II, requested by the US Army, was a version that saw limited use with the Marine Corps. The LVT-2(A) had a factory-installed armor plating on the hull and cab to resist heavy enemy machine-gun fire. This LVT version appeared identical to the Water Buffaloes except for the armored drivers' hatches. With armor fortification, the Buffalo IIs could function as assault vehicles in the lead waves of an amphibious landing. When introduced to the Marine operations on New Britain, these armored amphibious vehicles provided an excellent service.

Over 3,000 LVT-2(A)s and LVT-2s were manufactured during World War II. These combat vehicles were valuable assets to the Marine amphibious assault teams throughout the Pacific. They transported thousands of troops and tons of equipment. Still, the LVTs had overall design and operational deficiencies. For example, the vehicles lacked a ramp: all troops and equipment had to be loaded and unloaded over the gunwales. This caused problems in regular use and was hazardous during an enemy opposed landing.

This would be one of the leading factors to further develop amphibian tractors in the LVT family during the war.

SHERMAN MEDIUM TANKS

THE 2ND MARINE Division was assigned one company of M4-A2 Sherman medium tanks for Operation Galvanic. The fourteen tanks were deployed from Noumea in November 1943, onboard the *Ashland*. They joined Task Force 53 en route to the Gilberts. Each of these 34-ton, diesel-powered Sherman tanks were operated by a crew of five. They had a gyro-stabilized 75mm gun and three machine guns. Marines had no opportunity to train or operate with their new offensive assets until the D-Day chaos on Betio.

The medium Sherman tanks joined Wave 5 of the ship-to-shore assault on Betio. The tanks weaved through the gauntlet of Japanese fire without incident. Five were damaged when they plunged into hidden shell craters in the murky water. Onshore, the Marines' lack of operating experience with medium tanks proved costly to the remaining Shermans. Commanders ordered the tanks inland to attack targets of opportunity, unsupported. All but two tanks were quickly knocked out of action. Salvage crews worked non-stop each night, stripping severely damaged tanks to keep the others operational.

The Marines had now learned to use these tanks with an integrated team of covering infantry and engineers. With these new tactics, the Sherman's proved invaluable to Major Ryan's seizure of Green Beach on D+1, attacks on D+2, and the final assault on D+3. Early in the fight, Japanese 75mm anti-tank guns were deadly to the Shermans. But once these enemy weapons were neutralized, the defenders could do little more than shoot out the periscope with sniper fire.

Col. Shoup was disappointed by the squandered deployment and heavy losses of the Shermans on D-Day but was tempered by a subsequent admiration for their tactical role onshore. Shoup also wrote that the "so-called crushing effective medium tanks, as a tactical measure, was negligible in the operation." He believed that no one should place any faith in eliminating fortifications by running them over with a tank.

Marine commanders agreed that the Shermans rendered their light tanks obsolete. Medium tanks were easier to get ashore, and they packed greater armor and firepower. By the war's end, the American ordinance industry had manufactured over 48,000 medium Sherman tanks for use by the Marine Corps and US Army in all combat theaters.

OPERATION BACKHANDER

1944 BATTLE FOR CAPE GLOUCESTER

INTRODUCTION

Early on the morning of December 26, 1943, Marines stood ready off the coast of Japanese-dominated New Britain. The outline of the mile-high Mount Talawe was just visible in the twilight. American and Australian cruisers shattered the early morning calm with ammunition flying from their destroyers' guns. The 1st Marine Division, was commanded by Major General William H. Rupertus, arriving from the recently finished Guadalcanal Campaign. The men steeled their nerves, waiting for daylight and the signal to assault the Yellow Beaches near Cape Gloucester.

Fire support ships blazed away for ninety minutes. They attempted to neutralize entire areas rather than destroy pinpointed targets because the dense jungle concealed most of the individual Japanese fortifications and ammunition dumps.

At dawn on D-Day, Army airmen joined the bombardment. B-24 Liberator bombers flew at such an altitude that the Marines could barely see them. They dropped five-hundred-pound bombs on the beaches, scoring a hit on one of the enemy fuel dumps at the Cape Gloucester airfield—releasing a fiery geyser that leapt hundreds of feet into the air. A squadron of B-25 medium bombers and A-20 light bombers followed them, attacking from a lower altitude, hammering the Japanese antiaircraft batteries.

US B-25 Mitchell Bombers

Then the attention shifted to the assault beaches. Landing craft carrying two battalions of the 7th Marines started toward the shore. An LCI (Landing Craft, Infantry), with multiple rocket launchers, took positions on the flank of the first wave bound for each beach. They unleashed a hellish barrage, keeping the Japanese troops pinned down after the destroyers and cruisers shifted their fire to avoid putting the assault troops in danger.

At 0745, Higgins boats brought the first wave toward Yellow Beach 1. They grounded onto a narrow strip of volcanic sand that measured just under five hundred yards from one end to the other, bringing the 3rd Battalion Marines' lead elements. Two minutes later, the 1st Battalion landed on Yellow Beach 2. Separated by a thousand yards of jungle and a seven-hundred-yard shoreline. Neither battalion encountered any organized resistance. The Marines used a smoke-screen that drifted across the beaches. This hampered the later waves of landing craft and blinded Japanese observers on Target Hill overlooking the beachhead. No enemy manned the log-and-earth bunkers that might have raked the assault force with deadly fire.

The Yellow Beaches on the north coast of the peninsula pointed west toward Cape Gloucester. Codenamed Operation Backhander, this access point was the primary objective: two airfields at the cape's northwestern tip. By capturing the airfields, the 1st Marine Division would allow Allied airmen to step up attacks on the Japanese fortress at Rabaul, three hundred miles away at the northeastern edge of New Britain —the opposite end of the long, crescent-shaped island. The capture of these Yellow Beaches was vital for the New Britain Campaign, but two additional landings also took place. The first occurred on December 15, landing at Cape Merkus on Arawe Bay along the south coast. The second at Green Beach on the northwest coast, also on December 26.

The Cape Merkus landing was across the channel from the islet of Arawe. Its purposes were to disrupt motorized barges and other Japanese small-craft moving men and supplies along the southern coast of New Britain and to divert attention from Cape Gloucester. The Marine amphibian tractor crews used the slower and more vulnerable LVT-1 Alligators and the new armored LVT-2 Water Buffaloes to carry soldiers from the 112th Cavalry to make landings on Orange Beach at the western edge of Cape Merkus.

The destroyer *Conyngham* provided fire support enhanced by rocket equipped DUKW's (a 2.5-ton, six-wheel, amphibious truck known as duck) and a submarine chaser designated as the control craft. A last-minute bombing silenced the beach defenses and enabled the LVT Water Buffaloes to crush enemy machine guns that survived the opening bombardment.

Two diversionary landings by soldiers paddling ashore in rubber boats were less successful. Savage enemy fire forced one group to turn back just short of its objective on Orange Beach, but the other gained a foothold on Pilelo Island and killed the small group of Japanese defenders. Enemy airmen reported the assault force approaching Cape Merkus. Japanese bombers and fighters from Rabaul attacked within two hours of the landing. The Japanese executed sporadic airstrikes throughout December with diminishing ferocity. They ultimately shifted their troops to meet the threat in the south.

Then there was the secondary landing on December 26. Battalion Landing Team 21 was a 1,500 man assault force, from the 2/1 Marines, commanded by Lieutenant Colonel James Masters. They started toward Green Beach supported by American destroyers *Smith* and *Reid* with their 5-inch naval gunfire. LCMs (Landing Craft, Medium) carried amphibian trucks, driven by soldiers, fitted with rocket launchers. They fired from the landing craft as the assault force attacked the beach. The first wave landed at 0750, with two others closely following ashore. The Marines carved out a beachhead 1,200 yards wide and 500 yards inland, encountering no opposition. Their mission was to sever the coastal trail that passed west of Mount Talawe and prevent Japanese from reinforcements reaching the Cape Gloucester airfields.

Following the coastal trail proved more difficult than expected. The local villagers tilled and cleared garden plots, leaving them for the jungle to reclaim. This left a maze of trails—some fresh, some faint—but most led nowhere. The Japanese did not take advantage of the confusion caused by the path tangling until early morning on December 30. They attacked the Green Beach force and took advantage of the heavy rain that muffled sounds and reduced visibility. When the Japanese began their assault, the Marines called down mortar fire within 20 yards of their defensive positions. A battery of the 11th Marines was reorganized as an infantry unit because the cannoneers couldn't find suitable targets for their 75mm howitzers.

Gunnery Sergeant Guiseppe Guilano materialized at critical moments and fired a light machine gun from his hip. His bravery and cool disdain for danger earned him a Navy Cross. While some Japanese troops penetrated the position, a counterattack led by Company G drove them off. This brutal fighting cost the Marines six dead and seventeen wounded. Ninety Japanese soldiers perished, and five surrendered.

ESTABLISHING THE BEACHHEAD

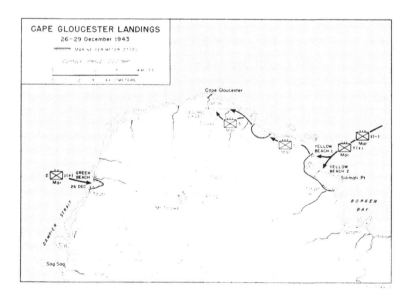

THE JAPANESE HAD a mixture of combat and service troops in western New Britain. They used motorized barges to shuttle cargo and troops along the coast from Rabaul to Cape Gloucester. They utilized their fleet of trawlers and schooners enhanced by destroyers from the Japanese Navy for any more extended movements.

Japanese troops that defended western New Britain were known as the *Matsuda Force*. General Iwao Matsuda was a military transportation specialist and a commander of an infantry regiment in Manchuria. When he arrived in February 1943 on New Britain, he took control of the battle-tested *141st Infantry* from the Philippines conquest and additional antiaircraft and artillery units. Matsuda established his headquarters near Kalingi, the coastal trail northwest of Mount Talawe, five miles from the airfields at Cape Gloucester. He ultimately changed his location to reflect his tactical challenges.

The Allies increased their threat to New Britain as 1943 wore on. Japanese headquarters at Rabaul assigned Gen. Matsuda's force to the *17th Division* under Lieutenant General Sakai, recently arriving from Shanghai. Sakai's division was attacked en route and lost two of their four transports to submarine torpedoes and mines. An Allied air attack nearly wiped out the third convoy. This deprived the Japanese defenders of three thousand replacement and service troops. LtGen. Sakai deployed the remainder of his forces to western New Britain under Matsuda's tactical command.

The mid-December Cape Merkus landings caused Gen. Matsuda to shift his troops to combat the threat. This redeployment did not account for the lack of resistance at the Yellow Beaches. Matsuda was familiar with the terrain of western New Britain. He did not believe the Americans would storm the small strips of sand that extended a few yards inland, backing up to a swamp. Matsuda did not know the American maps labeled the beaches as a "swamp forest." Even though the aerial photography taken after the initial preliminary airstrikes revealed no shadow within the bomb craters—there was evidence of a water level high enough to fill these depressions to the brim. Matsuda knew the airfields were the obvious prize and did not believe that the Marines would plunge into the muck and risk becoming bogged down short of achieving their objective.

Matsuda forfeited the immediate advantage of opposing the Marine assault force at the water's edge. Enemy troops were suffering the long-term indirect effects of eroding Japanese fortunes, beginning at Guadalcanal and New Guinea. The Allies dominated the skies over New Britain, blunted any air attacks on the beach at Cape Merkus beachhead, and bombed at will throughout the island. While the airstrikes did minor damage, except for Rabaul, they demoralized the Japanese troops suffering from medicine and supply shortages because of the submarine and air attacks. An ineffective network of primitive trails hugged the coastline and increased Gen. Matsuda's dependence on barges. The capture of Cape Merkus made his barges, convoys, and coastal shipping vulnerable to aircraft, and later to gunboats and torpedo craft.

The two battalions that landed on the Yellow Beaches crossed the sands and plunged through a wall of undergrowth into a swamp forest. A Marine could slog through knee-deep mud, step into a hole, and then end up damp to his neck. A Japanese counterattack while the Marines lurched through the swamp forest could have inflicted severe casualties. Gen. Matsuda lacked the roads and vehicles to shift his troops in time to take advantage of the terrain. The Japanese defenders were immobile on the ground and tried to retaliate by air. A flight of enemy aircraft sent from Rabaul was intercepted by Army P-38s. Two Japanese bombers evaded the Army fighter planes and sank the destroyer *Brownson* with a direct hit, followed by an immense explosion. She took 108 crewmen with her; the rest were rescued by destroyers *Daly* and *Lamson*.

When the first Japanese bombers came into view, a squadron of Army B-25s flew over LSTs (Landing Ships, Tank) attacking targets at Borgen Bay, south of the Yellow Beaches. Gunners on board the LSTs opened fire at the enemy aircraft but mistook friend for foe and shot down two American bombers and damaged two others. The Allied planes, shaken by the experience, dropped their bombs too soon on the 11th Marines' artillery positions at the left flank of Yellow Beach 1—killing one Marine and wounding fifteen others. A Marine battalion commander from the artillery regiment later wrote:

> *It was like trying to dig a hole with my nose as the bombs exploded. Trying to get down into the ground just a little bit more.*

By the afternoon of D-Day, the 1st Marine Division had established a beachhead. The 7th Marines' assault battalions had pushed ahead and captured Target Hill on the left flank before pausing to await reinforcements. Two more battalions arrived during the day: Landing Team 31 came ashore at 0815 on Yellow Beach 1. They weaved through the 3/7 Marines and veered to the northwest, leading the way toward the airfields at 0845. The 2/7 Marines landed and waded through the swamp forest between the 1st and 3rd Battalions, expanding the beachhead. The next infantry unit was the 1/1 Marines, reaching Yellow Beach 1 at 1300 to join the 3rd Battalion advancing on the airfields. The 11th Marines, despite the accidental bombing, set up their artillery with the help of amphibian tractors. Some of the amphibious tractors brought the 75mm howitzers from the LSTs directly to the battery firing positions. Other tractors were used to break a trail through the undergrowth to pull the more massive 105mm weapons.

Army trucks loaded with supplies came ashore from the LSTs. Logistical plans called for these vehicles to move forward as mobile supply dumps, but the swamp forest proved impossible for the wheeled vehicles. Drivers abandoned their trucks to avoid being left behind when the ships moved out from the threat of Japanese bombers. The Marines built roads and corduroyed them with logs or shifted the cargo onto the amphibian tractors. Even with this enormous effort, the convoy still got underway with over 100 tons of supplies left on board.

While the cargo and reinforcements crossed the beach, the Marines advanced inland and encountered the first real Japanese resistance. On December 26 at 1015, the 3/1 Marines pushed ahead, forced into a column of companies by a swamp on the left flank that narrowed the frontage.

The Japanese opened fire from camouflaged bunkers, killing the commander of Company K and his executive officer. These sturdy Japanese bunkers proved impervious to the bazooka rockets, which failed to detonate in the soft earth covering the structures. And the 37mm guns could not penetrate the logs protecting the Japanese defenders.

An LVT-1 Alligator that had delivered supplies for Company K attempted to crush one bunker—but got wedged between two trees. Japanese snipers killed the tractor's two machine gunners before the driver could break it free. When the tractor lunged ahead, it caved in one bunker, silencing enemy fire and enabling Marines to isolate the three others and destroy them—killing twenty-five Japanese. A platoon of M4 Sherman tanks joined in to lead the advance beyond this first strongpoint.

Japanese troops of the *1st Debarkation Unit* provided the initial opposition, but Gen. Matsuda had alerted his nearby infantry units to converge onto the beachhead. A Japanese battalion moved into position late in the afternoon on D-Day. They were opposite the 2/7 Marines who clung to a crescent-shaped position with both flanks protected by marshlands.

After sunset, only muzzle flashes pierced the darkness as the firing intensity increased. The Japanese were preparing to counterattack. Amphibian tractors could not make supply runs until it was light enough to avoid the fallen tree trunks and roots when navigating through the swamp forest. Before dawn, Lieutenant Colonel "Chesty" Puller, the XO of the 7th Marines, organized the men of the service company and regimental headquarters into carrying parties. He loaded them with ammunition and waded with them through the dangerous swamp. Only one misstep and a Marine carrying bandoliers of rifle ammo or containers of mortar shells could slip, stumble, and drown.

When the regimental commander reinforced the Marines with Battery D, of the 1st Special Weapons Battalion, LtCol. Puller had the men leave the 37mm guns behind and carry the ammunition instead. A guide from headquarters met the column that LtCol. Puller had pressed into service. He led the Marines forward through a blinding downpour, driven sideways by a monsoon gale. Obscured landmarks forced the heavily laden Marines to blindly wade onward. Each man clung to the belt of the man in front. Not until 0805, over twelve hours after the column started its march, did the Marines reach their goal, put down their loads, and take up their rifles to fight.

The 2/7 Marines had been fighting for their lives since the first storm struck. A curtain of rain prevented mortar crews from seeing their aiming stakes. The battalion commander described these men firing as just "guessing by God's will." Mud got into most of the small arms ammo and jammed machine guns and rifles. Marines abandoned their water-filled foxholes while the defenders hung on fighting.

At dawn, Japanese soldiers moved toward the right flank

of the 2/7 Marines, attempting to outflank them. They were possibly forced into that direction by the Marines' defensive fire. When Battery D arrived and moved into the threatened area, they forced the Japanese to break off their action and regroup.

DEFENSE OF HELL'S POINT

THE OVERALL PLAN for the 1st Division Marines' maneuver called for Combat Team C to take and hold a beachhead at Target Hill. Combat Team B would advance on the airfields. Due to the enemy build-up to prepare for the attack, Gen. Rupertus requested the release of the division reserve, Combat Team A, to reinforce the Marines. The Army agreed and sent the 1st, 2nd, and 3rd Battalions in support.

The division commander landed them on Blue Beach, three miles right of the Yellow Beaches. By using Blue Beach, this placed the 5th Marines closer to Cape Gloucester and the airfields. Not every element of Combat Team A received these orders. Several units touched down on the Yellow Beaches instead and moved on foot to their planned destination.

While Gen. Rupertus laid out plans to commit the reserve troops, Combat Team B advanced toward the airfields. Marines initially encountered light resistance but were warned of a maze of trenches and bunkers stretching inland from a promontory—earning the name Hell's Point. Japanese troops built these defenses to protect the beaches where Gen. Matsuda had expected the Allies to land. The 3/1 Marines attacked the Hell's Point position on the flank instead of a head-on frontal assault. Overrunning this complex set of defenses proved a lethal task.

Rupertus delayed the attack to give the division reserve, the 5th Marines, time to come ashore. On December 28, after the 2/11 Marines and Army A-20s bombarded the dug-in enemy, the assault troops suffered another delay. They waited several hours for a platoon of M4 Sherman medium tanks to increase the attack's intensity. At 1100, the 3/1 Marines moved ahead. Company I and the medium Sherman's led the way. At the same time, Company A waded through jungle and swamp intending to seize the ridge's inland point extending from Hell's Point. Despite the obstacles in their path, Company A surged from the jungle at 1145, crossing the tall grass field until repulsed by intense enemy fire. By late afternoon, Company A broke off the attack. Attackers and defenders were short of ammunition and exhausted. The 2/11 Marines covered Company A's withdrawal behind an onslaught of fire. By nightfall, the Japanese had abandoned their positions.

The attached Shermans with Company I collided head-on with the primary defenses fifteen minutes after Company A assaulted inland of the ridge. The Japanese had modified their defenses since the December 26 landings. They hacked fire lanes in the undergrowth, cut new gun ports and bunkers, and moved men and weapons to oppose the Allied attack along the coastal trail parallel to the shore instead of over the beach. The Marines advanced in drenching rain and encountered jungle-covered enemy positions protected by mines and barbed wire.

Medium Sherman tanks, protected by riflemen, crushed the bunkers and weapons inside. Company I drifted to the left flank during the fight, and Company K, reinforced with a platoon of Sherman tanks, closed the gap between the coastal track and Hell's Point. This unit used the same tactics as Company I. A rifle squad followed each of the Shermans after the tanks cracked the twelve bunkers and fired inside. The riflemen killed anyone attempting to fight or flee. Nine Marines were killed and thirty-six were wounded in this assault while over two hundred and sixty Japanese died fighting.

After the Marines shattered the Hell's Point defenses, two battalions of the 5th Marines joined in the airfield's advance. The 1st and 2nd Battalions moved out in a column. In front of the Marines was a swamp only a few inches deep. The downpour increased the depth to over five feet making it hard for the shorter Marines. The 5th Marines lost time wading through the swamp. This delayed the attack while the leading elements chose a piece of open and dry ground to establish a perimeter while the remaining Marines caught up.

The 1/1 Marines encountered only scattered resistance— mostly sniper fire—as they weaved along the coast beyond Hell's Point. Advancing with half-tracks carrying 75mm guns, artillery, medium Sherman's, and even rocket-firing DUKWs, the 1st Marines held a line extended inland from the coast. The 3/1 Marines and the 2/5 Marines advanced on the flanks and formed a semicircle around the airfield.

Colonel Sumiya of the *53rd Infantry Regiment* was the Japanese officer in charge of defending the airfields. On December 29, he fell back to gain time. Sumiya gathered the surviving troops for Razorback Hill's defense, a ridge running diagonally across the southwestern approaches to the airfield. The 5th Marines attacked on December 30, supported by artillery and tanks. Sumiya's troops had built sturdy bunkers, but the chest-high grass covering Razorback Hill did not stop the Allied assault like the jungle at Hell's Point. The Imperial Japanese fought bravely to hold their position, even stalling the Marines' advance. But the Japanese had neither the firepower nor the numbers to overcome. During the Japanese assault, one platoon of Company F beat back three *banzai* attacks.

Medium Shermans allowed the Marines to smash the remaining bunkers in their path and kill the enemy troops within. By nightfall on December 30, the Marine landing force overran the airfield defenses. At noon the next day, Gen. Rupertus hoisted the American flag next to the wreckage of a Japanese bomber at Airfield No. 2—the larger of the airstrips.

The 1st Marine Division seized the objective for the Battle of Cape Gloucester. But the airstrips proved only marginal value to the Allies. Airfield No. 1 was overgrown with sharp, tall kunai grass. Craters from American bombs pockmarked the surface of Airfield No. 2. After its capture, Japanese hit-and-run planes added more bomb craters, despite antiaircraft fire from the 12th Defense Battalion. Army aviation engineers worked desperately around the clock to get Airfield No. 2 back in operation. This task took until the end of January 1944. Army aircraft based here defended against air assaults for as long as Rabaul remained an active Japanese airbase.

CROSSING SUICIDE CREEK

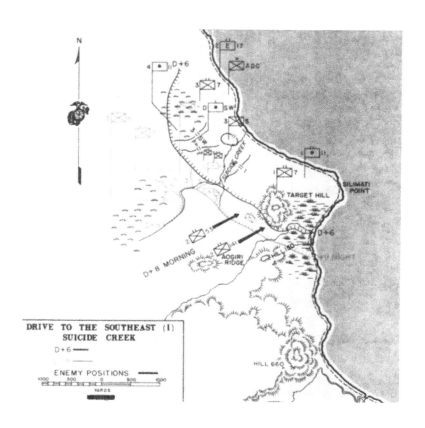

DRIVE TO THE SOUTHEAST (I)
SUICIDE CREEK

D + 6

ENEMY POSITIONS

1000   500   0   500   1000
YARDS

TARGET HILL

SILIMATI POINT

AOGIRI RIDGE

D + 8 MORNING

HILL 660

Wʜɪʟᴇ Mᴀᴊᴏʀ Gᴇɴᴇʀᴀʟ Rupertus directed the airfields' capture, Brigadier General Lemuel Shepherd had come ashore on December 26 and took command of the beachhead. Shepherd had coordinated the logistics activity and assumed responsibility to expand the perimeter southwest and secure Borgen Bay's shores. He used a shore party of engineers, transportation, and service troops to handle the logistics. The 3/5 Marines arrived on December 30 to help the 7th Marines enlarge the beachhead.

Gen. Shepherd had limited knowledge of the Japanese deployments to the south and west of the Yellow Beaches. Thick vegetation concealed swamps, streams, ridgelines, trenches, and bunkers. The progress made toward the airfields showed a Japanese weakness in that area and a potential strength in Borgen Bay and the Yellow Beaches vicinity. To resolve the uncertainty of the enemy's intentions and numbers, Gen. Shepherd issued orders to probe enemy defenses on January 1, 1944.

Colonel Katayama commanded the *141st Infantry* and prepared a counterattack. Katayama intended to hurl three reinforced battalions against the Allies at Target Hill. Japanese headquarters believed 2,500 Marines were now ashore on New Britain, 10% of the total. Col. Katayama thought his force was strong enough to do this job.

Katayama waited and gathered his strength, giving Gen. Shepherd time to make the first move. Midmorning on January 2, the 1/7 Marines stood ready near Target Hill. The 2nd Battalion waited along a stream known as Suicide Creek. The 3/5 Marines advanced into the jungle to cover the 3/7 Marines on one flank. As the units pivoted, they would cross Suicide Creek to squeeze out of the 2/7th Marines and provide Shepherd with a reserve.

The change in direction through thick vegetation proved exceptionally difficult. In the words of one Marine:

You'd step from your line, take ten paces, and turn around to guide your buddy, and nobody was there. I can tell you it was a very small war and a very lonely business.

The Japanese troops were dug in south of Suicide Creek. From there, they resisted every attempt by the Marines to cross the stream that day. This created a stalemate until Seabees from Company C built a corduroy road. They punched through the swamp forest behind the Yellow Beaches for the tanks to move forward and smash through enemy defenses.

While Marines waited at Suicide Creek on Sherman tanks, Katayama attacked Target Hill. He took advantage of the darkness. His infantry cut steps into the lower slopes so troops could climb more efficiently. The Japanese followed their preconceived plan, to the letter, of advancing up the steps and slipping past the Company A, 7th Marines' thinly held lines. At midnight enemy troops stormed the strongest of the company's defenses. Japanese mortars fired to soften the defenses and screen the approach. Still, they could not conceal the sound of the soldiers working their way up the hill, and the Marines were ready. While Japanese supporting fire proved to be inaccurate, one round did score a direct hit on a machine gun position killing the gunner and wounding two others. The injured Marines kept on firing their weapon until someone else could take over. This lone gun fired over five thousand rounds and helped stop the Japanese thrust, ending at dawn. The Japanese could not crack the 1/7 Marines' lines or loosen their grip on Target Hill.

A dead Japanese officer on Target Hill had documents that cast a new light on enemy defenses south of Suicide Creek. On a crudely drawn map, Aogiri Ridge was discovered. This enemy strongpoint was unknown to Gen. Shepherd's intelligence section. Observers on Target Hill searched for the Aogiri Ridge trail network, but the jungle canopy frustrated their efforts.

Marine patrols on Target Hill found dozens of enemy bodies. They captured documents that, when translated, listed forty-seven killed Japanese and fifty-five wounded. Using field glasses to scan the jungle south of Suicide Creek, the 17th Marines finished the road to allow the Sherman tanks to test the stream's defenses.

On the afternoon of January 3, three Sherman tanks reached the creek. They realized the bank dropped off too sharply for them to negotiate. The engineers called in a bulldozer; they lowered its blade to gouge out the lip of the embankment. The Japanese realized the danger if the tanks could cross the creek and opened fire on the bulldozer, wounding the driver. A Marine climbed into the exposed driver seat until he was also wounded. Another Marine jumped forward, but instead of climbing onto the machine, he walked alongside and used its bulk for cover. He manipulated the controls with an ax handle and a shovel. By dark, he'd finished the job of converting the impossible bank into a ramp the Shermans could cross.

At dawn on January 4, the first Sherman went down the ramp and across the stream. As the tank emerged on the other side, Marines cut down two Japanese soldiers trying to detonate mines against the tank's sides. Other Shermans followed, accompanied by infantry, and smashed open the bunkers barring the way. The 3/7 Marines surged across the creek and joined the other battalions on the far right of the line that crossed the jungle, concealing Japanese defenses at Aogiri Ridge.

Now across Suicide Creek, the Marines advanced on Aogiri Ridge, another name for Hill 150. The Marine advance rapidly took the hill, but the Japanese resistance in the vicinity did not stop. Enemy fire wounded the commanding officer of the 3/5 Marines and killed his executive officer. On the morning of January 8, Lieutenant Colonel Lewis W. Walt, the executive officer of the 5th Marines, took command of the 3rd Battalion. Walt continued the attack from the previous day. His Marines encountered savage fire, and through the thick jungle they moved up a steep slope. The battalion formed a perimeter and dug in as night approached. Sudden skirmishes and random Japanese fire punctuated the darkness. The determined resistance and nature of the terrain convinced LtCol. Walt that he had a fight on his hands for Aogiri Ridge.

Drenching rain, mud, and rampaging streams blunted the shock action and firepower of the tanks. The heaviest weapon the Marines could bring forward was a 37mm gun. The 11th Marines hammered the crest of Aogiri Ridge while the 7th Marines probed the flanks. The 3/5 Marines advanced in the center, seizing a narrow segment of the slope. By nightfall, LtCol. Walt reported that his men had "reached the limit of their physical endurance and morale was low. It was now a question of whether they could hold their hard-earned gains."

The Marine crew of the 37mm gun opened fire to support the afternoon's last attack. After only two rounds, four of the nine men handling the weapon were wounded. LtCol. Walt called for volunteers. When no one responded, he crawled to the gun and pushed the weapon up the incline. After firing two more rounds and cutting a swath to the undergrowth, his third-round destroyed an enemy machine gun. From there, other Marines took over, and the new volunteers cut down the enemy. The new 37mm improvised gun crew continued to fire canister rounds every few yards until they manhandled the weapon to the crest. From there, the Marines dug in 10 yards away from bunkers the Japanese had built on the crest of the reverse slope.

At 0130 on January 10, the Japanese charged through a curtain of rain, firing and shouting as they attacked. The Marines clinging to the ridge repelled this attack and the three others that followed, costing the Marines nearly all of their ammunition. Marine reinforcements scaled the muddy slope with clips and belts of ammo for the machine guns and rifles. Still, there was hardly any time to distribute the ammunition before the Japanese launched their fifth attack of the morning. Marine artillery decimated the enemy as the forward observers' vision was obstructed by rain and jungle; fire was adjusted by sounds more than sight. They moved the 105mm concentration to within fifty yards of the Marine infantrymen.

A Japanese officer emerged from the darkness and ran toward LtCol. Walt's foxhole before fragments of a shell bursting in the trees cut him down. This was the climax of the enemy counterattack at Aogiri Ridge. The Japanese tide receded as daylight grew brighter. When the Marines moved forward at 0800, they did not find one living Japanese at Aogiri Ridge—now renamed Walt's Ridge in honor of their commander, who received the Navy Cross for his heroic leadership.

Only one Japanese stronghold in the vicinity of Walt's Ridge still survived. A supply dump along the trail linking the ridge to Hill 150. On January 11, the 1/7 Marines accompanied by two half-tracks and a platoon of light tanks eliminated the enemy resistance in four hours of fighting. It had been fifteen days of combat since the landings on December 26. It cost the division 182 killed and 640 wounded.

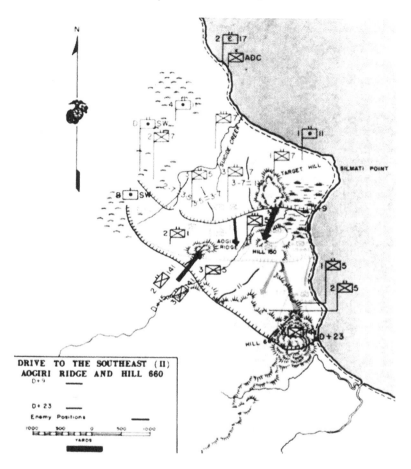

DRIVE TO THE SOUTHEAST (II)
AOGIRI RIDGE AND HILL 660

D+9

D+23

Enemy Positions

1000   500   0   500   1000

YARDS

The next objective was Hill 660. It was to the left of Gen. Shepherd's zone of action and inland of the coastal track. The 3/7 Marines got orders to seize the hill. Captain Joseph W. Buckley, commander of the 7th Marines Weapons Company, created a task force to bypass Hill 660 and block the coastal trail beyond the objective.

Buckley used two platoons of infantry, a platoon of 37mm guns, two half-tracks, and two light tanks. He assigned a platoon of pioneers from the 17th Marines with the bulldozer to trail the task force. They pushed through the mud and set up a roadblock to block the line of retreat from Hill 660. The Japanese attacked with long-range, plunging fire against Capt. Buckley's task force as it advanced one mile along the trail. Because of the flat trajectory, the 37mm and 75mm guns could not destroy the enemy's automatic weapons. But the Marines succeeded in forcing enemy gunners to keep their heads down. As they advanced, Buckley's task force unreeled telephone wire to keep in contact with headquarters. Once the roadblock was in place and camouflaged, Buckley requested a truck bring in hot meals for his men. When the truck got bogged down—he sent the bulldozer to pull it free.

Buckley called in an aerial bombardment and artillery fire at 0930 on January 13. His tanks could not negotiate the ravines on the hillside. The climb became so steep that the riflemen had to sling their arms and seize handholds along the vines to pull themselves up. This is when the Japanese suddenly opened fire from trenches at the crest and pinned down the Marines climbing toward them. The Marines responded with mortar fire to silence the enemy lacking an overhead cover. Capt. Buckley's riflemen followed closely behind the mortar barrage and scattered the defenders. Many trying to escape along the coastal trail were shot down by the task force waiting for them.

Because of the torrential rain, the Japanese did not coun-terattack until January 16. Two companies of Katayama's troops charged up the southwestern slope and were slaugh-tered by small arms and mortar fire. Of the enemy lucky enough to survive and try to break through the roadblock, forty-eight perished.

After the capture of Hill 660, the nature of the campaign changed. The Allies had captured their objective and elimi-nated any possibility of a Japanese counterattack against the airfield. Now the Marines would repel the Japanese, who harassed the secondary beachhead at Cape Merkus. Marines would also secure the jungle-covered mountainous interior of Cape Gloucester—south of the airfields between the Yellow and Green beaches.

MOPPING UP IN THE WEST

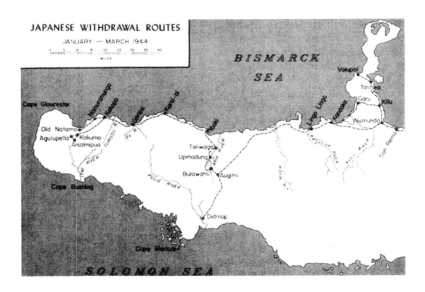

JAPANESE WITHDRAWAL ROUTES
JANUARY — MARCH 1944

THE FIGHTING at Cape Merkus on the south coast of western New Britain paled compared to Cape Gloucester's savage struggle. Japanese in the south were content to take advantage of the dense jungle and contain the 112th Cavalry on Cape Merkus. The Japanese commander, Major Komori, believed that the Allied landing force's plan was to capture an abandoned airfield at Cape Merkus. Komori built Japanese defenses to protect the airfield. He created a series of concealed bunkers with integrated fields of fire to hold the lightly armed cavalrymen in check while his troops directed harassing fire toward the beach.

The 112th Cavalry unit lacked heavy weapons. They called for 1st Marine Division tanks left behind on Finschhafen, New Guinea, because the other tanks were already turning up the mud at Cape Gloucester. Eighteen M5A1 light tanks from Company B of the 1st Marine Tank Battalion answered the call. They arrived at Cape Merkus and moved into position on January 15. The tanks attacked the next day after a squadron of Army B-24s dropped one-thousand-pound bombs on enemy jungle-covered defenses. The Marines followed up with artillery and mortars, joining in on the bombardment after two platoons of tanks and two infantry companies charged ahead.

Some tanks bogged down in the rain-soaked soil, and tank retrievers were needed to pull them free. Despite the nearly impenetrable thickets and deep mud, the tank infantry teams destroyed most of the Japanese bunkers. After eliminating the source of the harassing fire, the Allied troops pulled back. They destroyed a tank immobilized by a thrown track so the enemy could not create a pillbox. Another tank trapped in a crater was nearly destroyed—but Army engineers were able to free it and bring it back to service.

The January 16 attack broke the back of remaining Japanese resistance. Maj. Komori ordered a retreat to the vicinity of the airstrip, but the 112th Cavalry launched an attack that caught and shot them to pieces. By the time the Japanese dug in to defend the airfield—which the Americans had no intention of seizing—Komori's men lost 116 dead and 117 wounded with another 94 too sick to fight. Through starvation and sickness, the Japanese hung on until February 24, when Maj. Komori received orders to join the *Matsuda Force* in a general retreat.

On the other side of the island, after the victories at Hill 660 and Walt's Ridge, the 5th Marines focused on seizing control of the Borgen Bay shore's to the east of Yellow Beach 2. The 1/5 Marines followed the coastal trail until January 20, when the column smashed into a Japanese stronghold at Natamo Point. Documents captured earlier in the fighting described one enemy platoon supported by automatic weapons as dug in. Allied airstrikes and artillery could not suppress the enemy fire. The seized documents proved to be out of date when at least one company armed with 20mm, 37mm, and 75mm weapons stalled the Allied advance.

Marine reinforcements called in Sherman tanks that arrived in LSTs on January 23. That afternoon, supported by rocket firing DUKWs and artillery, the Marines overran Natamo Point. The battalion commander dispatched patrols along the west bank of the Natamo River. They outflanked strong enemy positions on the east bank near the stream's mouth. While the Marines executed this maneuver, the Japanese abandoned their defenses and retreated to the east.

The success at Borgen Bay and Cape Gloucester enabled the 5th Marines to probe the trails leading inward toward the village of Magairapua, where Katayama once had his head-quarters. The 5th Marines led the way to trap enemy troops still bottled up on western New Britain.

Company L of the 1st Marines pursued the retreating Japanese from Cape Gloucester toward Mount Talawe. Marines crossed the mountain's eastern slope and weaved their way through a cluster of lesser outcroppings, through Mount Langila and into the saddle between Mounts Tangi and Talawe. They discovered four unoccupied bunkers situated to defend the track they'd followed, with another trail running east to west. Company L found the main route on the coast to the village of Agulupella from Sag Sag and ultimately onto Natamo Point on the northern coast.

Taking full advantage of this discovery, the 1st Marine patrol advanced south along the trail. At the same time, a composite company from the 7th Marines landed at Sag Sag on the West Coast and moved along an east-west track. Australian reserve officer, William Weidman, a former Episcopal missionary at Sag Sag, served as guide and contact for the natives. When enemy resistance stopped the 1st Marine patrol short of the trail junction near Mount Talawe, Company K of the 1st Marines attacked.

For three hours, the Marines of Company K tried to break through a line of bunkers concealed by jungle growth. The Marines took fifteen casualties and withdrew beyond the reach of the Japanese mortars. The Japanese broke from cover and pursued a brave but foolish move that exposed the enemy troops to a deadly fire. This vigorous pursuit along the coast and the inland trails failed to trap the Japanese. The Marines captured Gen. Matsuda's abandoned headquarters in the shadow of Mount Talawe. Inside they found documents buried instead of burned—possibly because the smoke would bring down artillery fire or airstrikes. The Japanese general and his troops escaped.

Gen. Shepherd believed that Matsuda was headed to the vicinity of Mount Talawe to the south. He organized a battalion of six rifle companies—nearly four thousand men—entrusted to Chesty Puller. This patrol would advance from Agulupella on the east-west track down to Government Trail. Then all the way to Gilnit, a village on the Itni River, inland of Cape Bushing on the southern New Britain coast. Before LtCol. Puller could advance, the intelligence section discovered that the enemy was retreating to the northeast toward

Rabaul. Gen. Shepherd detached the newly arrived 1/5 Marines. He reduced LtCol. Puller's force from almost 4,000 to 350 Marines for the jungle march to Gilnit.

During this trek, Puller's Marines depended on supplies dropped from Allied planes. Puller was also assigned 150 native bearers to carry rations and supplies. Air Force B-17s dropped tons of cargo. The patrol was only possible because of the supplies dropped from the sky. But this did little to ease the Marine discomfort of plodding through the mud.

Despite the air assistance, the march to Gilnit taxed Marine ingenuity and hardened them for future action. LtCol. Puller, who had led many patrols during the American intervention in Nicaragua, seemed in good spirits during this action. Division supply clerks, aware of Pullers' disdain for any creature comforts, were startled when they read his requisitions for hundreds of insect repellent bottles. Puller later wrote:

We were always soaked and everything we owned was likewise, and that lotion made the best damn stuff to start a fire with that you ever saw.

LtCol. Puller's Marines slogged toward Gilnit on the Itni River, killing seventy-five Japanese, capturing one straggler, and weapons and equipment odds and ends. One abandoned enemy pack contained an American flag, probably captured by a *141st Infantry* soldier during Japan's Philippine conquest. When the patrol reached Gilnit, they met no opposition. Puller's Marines made contact with an rmy patrol from Cape Merkus and then headed toward the northern coast on February 16.

On February 12, to the west, Company B of the 1st Marines boarded landing craft to cross the Dampier Strait to occupy Rooke Island, fifteen miles off the coast of New Britain. Division intelligence believed that the enemy garrison had departed. They were correct. The enemy withdrawal began on December 6, three weeks before the Cape Gloucester landings.

Colonel Sato and half of his *51st Reconnaissance Regiment* of 500 men sailed to Cape Bushing, where Sato led his command up the river and joined the main body of the *Matsuda Force* east of Mount Talawe. Instead of committing Sato's troops to the defense of Hill 660, Matsuda directed him to delay and harass the 1st and 5th Marines who converged on the inland trail net. Col. Sato succeeded in stalling the Marine patrols. He bought time for Matsuda's forces to retreat to the northern coasts with the *51st Reconnaissance Regiment* serving as the rearguard.

Once the Marines realized what Gen. Matsuda was up to, cutting their line of retreat became the highest priority. They withdrew the 1/5 Marines from the Puller patrol on the eve of the march toward Gilnit. On February 3, Gen. Shepherd realized the Japanese did not have the strength to mount a counterattack on the airfields and devoted all his resources to destroy retreating enemy troops. Shepherd chose the 5th Marines, now restored to three-battalion strength, to pursue the fleeing Japanese troops. While light aircraft scouted the coastal track, landing craft stood fast and waited to debark the regiment to cut off and destroy Gen. Matsuda's force. Bad weather stalled the 5th Marines. Clouds concealed the enemy from aerial observation while the boiling surf ruled out landings on several beaches. With over 5,000 Marines and Army troops, the Allies rotated their battalions and sent out fresh troops each day. They also used ten LCMs (Landing Craft, Mechanical) to leapfrog the retreating Japanese.

Marines were not called upon to make marches for more than two days in a row, with few exceptions. After a one day hike, they either remained at camp for three days or made the next jump by LCM. The 5th Marines expected a battle for the Japanese supply point at Iboki Point, but enemy troops dwindled. Instead of encountering resistance by a resolute and clever rearguard, the 5th Marines only found stragglers, most wounded or too sick to fight. Marines kept up pressure on retreating Japanese troops. On February 24, they took Iboki Point without loss or even one man wounded.

During this action, American amphibious forces seized Eniwetok and Kwajalein Atolls in the Marshall Islands. The Central Pacific offensive now gathered momentum. Allied carrier strikes proved Truk was too vulnerable to continue serving as a significant enemy naval base. Now conscious of the threat to their inner perimeter developing to the north, the Japanese pulled back the fleet units from Truk and aircraft from Rabaul. On February 19, two days after the Allies invaded Eniwetok, enemy fighters at Rabaul took off to challenge an American air raid. When the Japanese bombers returned the next day, not a single operational Japanese fighter remained at the airfields.

The defense of Rabaul now depended on ground forces. LtGen. Sakai, commander of the *17th Division*, received orders to not dig in near Cape Hoskins and instead move to Rabaul. Sakai assumed the supplies he'd positioned along the trail would enable at least the most spirited of Matsuda's troops to stay ahead of the Marines and reach the fortress.

What was left of the self-propelled barges could carry the remaining troops and heavy equipment needed to defend Rabaul. This retreat would be an ordeal for the Japanese. The 5th Marines had already showed how swiftly they could move by taking advantage of Allied controlled skies and coastal waters. A full two-week march separated the nearest of Matsuda soldiers from their destination. While attrition was heavy, those who could contribute the least to Rabaul's defenses fell by the wayside.

LANDINGS AT VOLUPAI

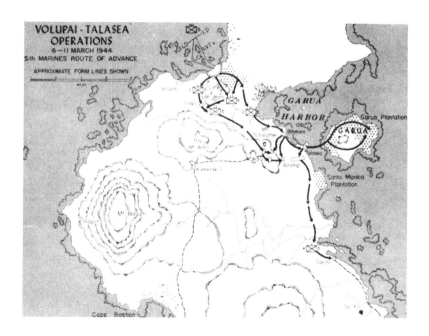

MARCH 6 WAS D-Day for the 5th Marines to land on the west coast of the Willaumez Peninsula—halfway between the base and the tip. Division intelligence believed that the Japanese strength between Talasea, site of the crude airstrip, and Cape

Hoskins, across Kimbe Bay were equal to the 5th Marines. Still, most of the enemy troops were defending Cape Hoskins. If the intelligence estimates were correct, Sakai prepared the last defense of Cape Hoskins before ordered to retreat to Rabaul.

A torpedo boat landed a recon team at Bagum. Their orders were to discover the intent of Japanese preparations near Volupai, nine miles from Red Beach, chosen for the assault. They learned Red Beach was lightly defended from native sources who'd worked at a plantation operated in the area before the war. The natives confirmed the Marine estimates of an enemy force of 600 men, two-thirds of them near Talasea, armed with artillery and mortars.

The Royal Australian Air Force, based out of Kiriwina Island to the south, bombed the Volupai region for three days. A force of 5th Marines, designated as Landing Team A, loaded into a small flotilla of landing craft set out from Iboki Point with an escort of torpedo boats.

On March 6, at 0835, the first amphibian tractors carrying assault troops clawed their way onto Red Beach. Sherman tanks in Army LCMs opened fire with machine guns. They waited to direct their 75mm weapons against any enemy gunner opposing the Allied landing force. Aside from difficult-to-pinpoint small arms fire, enemy opposition consisted mainly of mortar barrages, screened by the terrain. As Japanese mortar shells burst among the approaching landing craft, Captain Theodore A. Petras, flying a Piper L-4 Grasshopper, dove low over mortar positions and dropped hand grenades from the cockpit. Natives warned the Allied assault forces of a machine gun nest dominating the beach from the slopes on Little Mount Worri. The 1/5 Marines leading the way found it abandoned and encountered no serious opposition as they dug into protect the beachhead.

Four Sherman's supported the 5th Marines as they pushed farther inland, pressing their attack. One of the medium tanks got bogged down on Red Beach's soft sand, but the other three continued in a line. The lead tank lost momentum on a muddy rise, and two Japanese soldiers carrying landmines surged from cover to attack. Company E rifleman cut one down, but the other detonated his mine against the tank, killing himself and a Marine trying to stop him. The explosion jammed the tank's turret and stunned the crewmen inside, shaken but not wounded. The damaged Sherman moved aside to allow the other two tanks to pass, returning to the trail only to hit another mine.

After losing two tanks, one temporarily immobilized, and the other permanently out of action, the 5th Marines continued their advance. During the fighting at a Volupai coconut plantation, a dead Japanese soldier's body had a map showing the enemy positions around Talasea. By early afternoon, regimental intelligence distributed the information, which proved valuable for future operations.

Company E of the 5th Marines followed the trail to the plantation. At the same time, Company G kept pace, crossing the western shoulder of Little Mount Worri. Five P-39s from Airfield No. 2 at Cape Gloucester supported the attack. The pilots could not pinpoint the troops below and instead bombed Cape Hoskins, where there was no danger of hitting any Marines. Even without the aerial attack, the 2/5 Marines overran the plantation by nightfall and dug in for the night. Marines counted thirty-five Japanese killed.

Throughout the fighting, Combat Team A took eighty-four casualties. The artillery batteries suffered a more significant number of casualties than rifle companies.

The 2/11 Marines set up their 75mm howitzers on the open beach—exposed to fire from the 90mm mortars, which Capt. Petras showered with hand grenades. Some of the Navy Corpsmen on Red Beach, who helped the wounded artillerymen, ended up as casualties themselves. Thirty-four of the Marines killed and wounded on March 6 were members of the artillery unit. The gunners succeeded in registering their fires that afternoon and harassing the enemy through the night.

While the Marines prepared to renew their attack on the next day, the Japanese opposed them in order to keep a line of retreat open for the *Matsuda Force*. By doing so, the Japanese fell back from their prepared positions on the fringes of the Volupai plantation. This included the mortar pits that had caused such havoc with the 2/11 Marines. They dug in on the northern slopes of Mount Schleuther, overlooking the trail leading from the plantation to Bitokara village on the coast. Company F was sent uphill to disrupt the Japanese plan, while Company E remained on the trail to build up a base of fire.

On the right flank, Company F, the weapons platoon, surged from the undergrowth. They surprised Japanese machine gunners setting up their weapon, killing them, and turning the gun against the enemy troops. Company F's advance caught the Japanese in mid deployment and drove them back, killing over forty of their men. The 5th Marines established a night perimeter that extended from Mount Schleuther to the trail and embraced a portion of both.

The March 7 action was a departure from the plan. Originally, the 3/5 Marines would assume responsibility for the beachhead. Landing craft that had carried assault troops would depart from Red Beach on D-Day, and pick up the 3rd Battalion at Iboki Point, bringing them to Volupai. If the reinforcements were to arrive in time for an attack on the morning of March 7, this would require a dangerous nighttime Volupai approach through uncharted waters studded with sharp coral that could tear open the hull of the landing craft.

Gen. Shepherd decided the risks of such a move outweighed the advantages and canceled it at the last moment. No boats started the return voyage to Red Beach until after daylight on March 7, delaying Marine reinforcements until late afternoon. This left the 1st Battalion with only enough time to send Company C a short distance inland on the trail to the village of Liappo. When the trail petered out among trees and vines, Marines hacked their way forward until they ran out of daylight short of their objective.

The 1/5 Marines resumed the advance on March 8. Companies A and B moved through parallel paths leading east of Little Mount Worri.

Company A Marines peered through dense undergrowth and saw a figure in a Japanese uniform and opened fire. This man was a native wearing clothing discarded by the enemy and serving as a guide for Company B. The shots triggered an exchange of fire that killed two Marines, wounded the guide, and several others. Afterward, the advance resumed, but through formidable terrain—muddy ravines choked with brush and vines—which slowed the Marines as darkness fell with the battalion still on the trail.

The 2nd Battalion probed deeper into the enemy defenses. Patrols pushed ahead on the morning of March 8. They found Japanese troops dug in at the Bitokara Mission. The enemy fell back before the Marines could charge their position. Marines occupied Bitokara and advanced as far as Talasea taking over the abandoned airstrip. Other Marine patrols climbed the steep slopes of Mount Schleuther and collided with the enemy troops. Fire from a 90mm mortar, 75mm gun, and small arms killed eighteen Marines. Rather than press the attack in the darkness, Marines withdrew from the mountain and dug in at the Bitokara Mission. Mortars and artillery hammered the defenses through the night, leaving one company to defend the Talasea airstrip.

On the morning of March 9, Company G of the 2nd Marine Battalion advanced up Mount Schleuther while companies B and C cleared villages around the base. Company G expected to meet strong opposition during its part of the coordinated attack. But the Japanese had withdrawn from the mountaintop and left behind one artillery piece, two stragglers, and three dead. Enemy troops had festooned the abandoned 75mm gun with vines serving as tripwires for a booby-trap. When Marines hacked at the vines to examine the weapon more closely, they released the firing pins and detonated a round in the chamber. Since the Japanese gun crew had plugged the bore before they fled, the explosion ruptured the breach block and wounded several Marines.

After yielding the dominant terrain, the Japanese chose not to defend any of the villages clustered at the mountain's base. This opened up a route for the 5th Marines across the Willaumez Peninsula to support further operations against Gen. Matsuda's line of retreat. Since the March 6 offensive, the Allied force had killed an estimated 150 Japanese at the cost of seventeen dead and 114 wounded, most casualties taking place on the first day. The last phase of the fighting that began on Red Beach consisted of securing Garua Island, abandoned by the Japanese.

Results of the action at the base of the Willaumez Peninsula were mixed. The grassy Talasea airstrip lacked enough length to accommodate fighter planes. Still, the division's liaison planes made widespread use of it, landing on either side of a Japanese aircraft's carcass until the wreckage could be hauled away. The trail net was a web of muddy paths that required long hours of hard work by Company F of the 17th Marines. Army engineers used a 10-ton wrecker to recover three Sherman tanks that had become mired during the fighting. By March 10, the trails could support a further advance. Two days later, the 3/5 Marines provided a guard of honor. The same American flag flown over Airfield No. 2 on Cape Gloucester was raised over Bitokara.

FINAL COMBAT AND RELIEF

THE ALLIED FLOTILLA of Navy LCTs and Army LCMs supporting the Volupai landings continued to inflict damage on Japanese coastal traffic. On March 9, landing crafts carrying supplies around the tip of the peninsula spotted four enemy barges. They were beached and carelessly camouflaged. An LCT opened fire from its 20mm cannon and destroyed one of the Japanese barges. After that, two Army LCMs used their 37mm guns and opened fire on another barge beached on the shore.

The Japanese tried to make the best use of their shrinking number of barges, but the bulk of Gen. Matsuda's troops moved overland. A hundred Japanese were dug in at Garilli, but by the time Company K of the 3/5 Marines attacked on March 11, the Japanese had withdrawn to a new trail three miles away. Marines fought a series of actions lasting four days. The Japanese retreated a few hundred yards, dragging their 75mm gun that anchored each of the blocking positions. On March 16, Company K received 81mm mortars from an arriving LCM. The enemy turned their cannon seaward to deal with the threat but could not hit the landing craft. After the Marine mortars landed, they were quickly put into action. Japanese troops again withdrew, but this time they faded away since the bulk of Gen. Matsuda's force had escaped eastward.

The 5th Marines dispatched patrols southbound to the base of the Willaumez Peninsula, only capturing an occasional straggler, confirming the departure of Gen. Matsuda's primary force. The 1st Marine Division established training sites, a comfortable headquarters, and a hospital that used Japanese medicine stocks. Marines could swim in a rest area off the Garua beaches and hot springs ashore. The Navy then built a base on the Willaumez Peninsula for torpedo boats to harass surviving Japanese barges. On March 27, only the second day after the base was operating, Allied aircraft mistook two boats for enemy craft. They attacked—killing five and wounding eighteen sailors with friendly fire.

At the new training center on Garua, classes were taught to produce amphibious scouts for future operations. Headquarters decided that a reconnaissance of Cape Hoskins would be a suitable graduation exercise since aerial observers had seen no sign of enemy there. On April 13, sixteen trainees, two native guides, and a rifle platoon from the 2/5 Marines embarked on a pair of LCMs to Cape Hoskins. Two instructors stood by in one landing craft as the platoon established a trail block. Future scouts advanced toward the airfield at Cape Hoskins. The patrol encountered small arms and mortar fire en route to their objective. But the Marines had learned their lessons well, and they broke off the action and escaped with no casualties.

The Japanese had retreated. Maj. Komori's troops blazed the trail for Sato's command from Augitni to the northern coast. They encountered a dispiriting number of hungry stragglers as they marched toward Kandoka, a supply depot ten miles west of the Willaumez Peninsula. Komori's troops came under fire from an American landing craft as they crossed the Kuhu River. The rain-swollen river was a serious obstacle and became a detour that lasted two days until reaching a point where the stream narrowed.

On March 17, Komori's provisions ran out, forcing his troops to survive on birds, fish, and taro root, supplemented by coconuts from a nearby plantation. After losing a dozen men and additional time crossing the river, Komori's troops struggled into Kandoka. Only to discover that the food and other supplies had already been carried off to Rabaul. Maj. Komori pressed on through this crushing disappointment. His men continued to live off the land as best they could. Another five Japanese troops drowned in the fast-moving Kuhu River, and a native hired guide defected. Maj. Komori came down with a severe bout of malaria, and although physically weakened, he forced himself to continue.

Japanese survivors strived onward toward Cape Hoskins and ultimately into Rabaul. On Easter Sunday, 1944, a handful of half-starved enemy troops wandered onto the San

Remo Plantation, where Marines had bivouacked after pursuing Japanese troops eastward from the Willaumez Peninsula. The Marine unit was preparing to pass in review for the regimental commander when a sentry saw them and opened fire. The ensuing firefight killed three Japanese. One of the dead was Maj. Komori. In his pack was a rusty revolver and a diary that described the suffering of his command.

Col. Sato took the rest of the rearguard intended for the *Matsuda Force* and set out from Augitni on March 7. One day after Maj. Komori had sent word on the nineteenth that the 5th Marines' patrols had fanned out from the Willaumez Peninsula, where the reinforced regiment had landed two weeks earlier. When Sato reached Linga Linga he came across an abandoned Marine patrol bivouac. Sato's force had shrunk to less than 250 men, half the number he had starting out.

The following day, he was shocked when Allied landing craft appeared as his men prepared to cross the Kapaluk River. Sato set up a perimeter to repel the expected attack. The boats carried elements of the 2/1 Marines and landed a patrol from Company F on a beach beyond Kandoka. Another platoon was dispatched westward along the coastal track. Col. Sato was only aware of the landing's general location and groped eastward toward the village. On March 26, they collided. The Japanese surprised the Marines crossing a small stream and pinned them down for three hours until Company F reinforcements forced the Japanese to break off, take to the jungle, and bypass Kandoka.

Col. Sato's column disappeared into the jungle. One of the division's light airplanes scouting landing sites for the battalion sited the end of the column near Linga Linga. The Piper L-4 Grasshopper pilot sketched where the Japanese were and dropped the map to one of the troop-laden landing craft. The pilot then led the way to an undefended beach where the Marines waded ashore and set out to pursue Col. Sato and his troops. On March 30, an eight-man Marine patrol spotted a pair of Japanese with their rifles slung. These enemy troops were members of a seventy-three man patrol—too many to handle.

After the enemy column moved off, the eight-man patrol hurried back to Kandoka and reported. Outfitted with more machine guns, mortars, and men. This reinforced rifle platoon returned to the trail. The Japanese encountered another Marine patrol, which took up a position on high ground commanding the trail. When the reinforced rifle platoon heard gunfire, they hurried to aid the other Marines. The resulting slaughter killed fifty-five Japanese troops, including Col. Sato, who died, sword in hand, charging Marines. The Marines did not suffer one casualty during this encounter.

On April 9, the 3/1 Marines continued to search for enemy stragglers. The bulk of Gen. Matsuda's force, and whatever supplies it could transport, had retreated to Cape Hoskins.

Army troops were taking over for the Marines. It had now been four months since the landing at Cape Gloucester. The time had come for the amphibious forces to move on to an operation that would make better use of their specialized equipment and training. The last Marine action took place on April 22, when an ambush, sprung by the 2/5 Marines, killed twenty Japanese and caused the campaign's last Marine fatality. By seizing western New Britain as part of Rabaul's isolation, the division suffered 1,083 wounded and 310 killed in action—one-fourth of the Japanese casualties.

The capture of the Cape Gloucester airfields in early February 1944 tied down the 1st Marine Division for an extended period. This alarmed the recently appointed Commandant of the Marine Corps, Gen. Vandegrift. Referring to an extended engagement in New Britain, he wrote:

Six months there, and [the 1st Marine Division] will no longer be a well-trained amphibious division.

Vandegrift urged US Fleet Admiral Earnest King to help him pry the division from General Douglas MacArthur's grasp so he could again engage in amphibious operations. Admiral Nimitz, the commander-in-chief of Pacific Ocean Areas, requested the 1st Marine Division for the Palau Islands' impending invasion. The capture would protect MacArthur's flank on his advance to the Philippines.

Adm. Nimitz made the Army's 140th Infantry Division available to MacArthur. He swapped a division capable of taking over the New Britain Campaign for one that could spearhead the amphibious offensive against Japan. MacArthur briefly kept control of one Marine division, Company A, 1st Tank Battalion. The unit's medium tanks landed on April 22 at Hollandia on the northern coast of New Guinea. A swamp behind the beachhead stopped the Shermans from assisting the inland advance.

The commanding general of the Army's 140th Infantry Division was Major General Isaac R. Brush. He arrived on April 10 and arranged for the relief. His advance echelon landed on the 23rd, with the rest of the division following five days after. The 1st Marine Division departed on April 6 and May 4. They left behind the 12th Defense Battalion, who continued to provide antiaircraft defense for the Cape Gloucester airfields until replaced by an Army unit later in May.

The 1st Marine Division had plunged into an unforgiving jungle and overwhelmed a resolute enemy. They captured the Cape Gloucester airfields and drove the Japanese from western New Britain in just over four months. Several factors helped the Marines defeat the Japanese. The Allied control of the air and sea provided mobility. It disrupted the coastal barge traffic, which the enemy depended on for the movement of large quantities of medicine and supplies desperately needed for the retreat to Rabaul. Landing craft armed with rockets, aided by tanks and rocket-equipped amphibian trucks fired from landing craft, helped support the landings. But the size of the island and the lack of fixed coastal defenses reduced the efficiency of naval gunfire.

Marines defied the swamp and undergrowth by using superior engineering skills and bringing forward tanks that crushed enemy emplacements—adding to formidable American firepower. Through photo analysis, an art that improved rapidly, the Americans misinterpreted the nature of the swamp forest. However, Marine intelligence made excellent use of captured Japanese documents throughout the campaign. But it was the courage and endurance of the average Marine who made victory possible on Cape Gloucester. A Marine braved discomfort, disease, and violent death during his time in this hellish green Inferno.

MACARTHUR'S MARINES

GENERAL MACARTHUR WAS desperate for a trained amphibious unit to capture Rabaul. While the 1st Division Marines finished their rehabilitation in Australia, MacArthur approached the commander of the 6th Army, Lieutenant General Walter Kruger. MacArthur wanted to seize Rabaul and break the back of the Japanese resistance in the area. Worried about air cover for his amphibious operations, MacArthur planned to use the 1st Division Marines to capture the Cape Gloucester airfields. Allied aircraft based out of the captured airfields would support the 1st Division Marines assault on Rabaul.

The initial operational concept called for the conquest of western New Britain by storming Rabaul. He would split the 1st Marine Division by sending Combat Team A (5th Marines) against Gasmata on the island's southern coast. Combat team C (7th Marines) would seize the beachhead near the principal objective at Cape Gloucester's airfields. This would enable the Army's 503rd Parachute Infantry to exploit the Cape Gloucester beachhead. Combat Team B (1st Marines) would be held in reserve.

But revisions came swiftly in late October 1943. The new

plan now did not mention the capture of Rabaul. MajGen. Rupertus protested splitting Combat Team C. LtGen. Kruger decided to use all three battalions for the primary assault, substituting a battalion from Combat Team B for the West Coast landings. The airborne landing at Cape Gloucester would remain in the plan. But MajGen. Rupertus warned that foul weather could delay the drop and jeopardize Marine battalions already fighting ashore. This altered version earmarked Army troops for the landing on the southern coast.

Kruger's staff shifted the site from Gasmata to Arawe, a location closer to Allied airfields and farther from Rabaul's troops and aircraft. Combat Team B would put one battalion ashore southwest of the airfields. Two battalions of the 1st Marines would follow up on the assault at Cape Gloucester with Combat Team C. This left the division reserve, Combat Team A, to employ elements of the 5th Marines and reinforce the Cape Gloucester landings or conduct operations against the offshore islands to the west of New Britain.

During a December 14 briefing, only one day before the landings at Arawe, Gen. MacArthur asked how the Marines felt about the maneuver at Cape Gloucester. The division operations officer, Colonel Edwin A. Pollock, saw this opportunity to declare that the Marines objected to the plan. It depended on a speedy advance inland by a single reinforced regiment. To prevent heavy losses among the lightly armored paratroops, Pollock believed it would be better to bolster the amphibious forces than to try for an aerial envelopment that might fail or be delayed by the weather.

While he made no comment at the time, MacArthur may have heeded what Pollock said. Whatever the reason was, Kruger's staff eliminated the airborne portion and instructed the two battalions of the 1st Marines, still with Combat Team B, to land immediately after the assault waves. This would sustain the momentum of their attack and alert the division reserve to provide further reinforcements.

MAJOR GENERAL WILLIAM RUPERTUS

Born on November 14, 1889, in Washington DC, Rupertus's military career began in the District of Columbia National Guard. In 1910, he became a cadet in the US Revenue Cutter Service School, the Coast Guard Academy, in New London, Connecticut.

After being commissioned as a second lieutenant in the United States Marine Corps, he attended officer school and graduated first in his class in 1915. He commanded a Marine detachment aboard the USS Florida in World War I as a first lieutenant. After the war, he was promoted to captain and assigned to Haiti, where he gained experience in jungle fighting tactics.

He spent a year in the Army Command and General Staff School in Fort Leavenworth, Kansas. He was one of three Marines selected for that year and graduated with distinction. In 1929, he was given his first Far East assignment in Peking, China, and was promoted to major. Peking was quiet at the time, and while on duty, his first wife and two children died from a scarlet fever epidemic.

He returned to the War Plans Section at Headquarters in 1936 where he was appointed Chief of Staff of the Fleet Marine Force. After four years of service stateside, he returned to Shanghai, China as Executive Officer of the 4th Marines. There he became a lieutenant colonel. He witnessed the Japanese's brutal methods as they attempted to take over the International Settlement. Only with patience and discipline was a clash averted with the Japanese at that time.

After returning from China, Rupertus took command of the Marine Barracks in Washington DC, Guantánamo Bay, Cuba, and San Diego, California.

At the war's outbreak, Brigadier General Rupertus was the 1st Marine Division's assistant commander, training in New River, North Carolina, under Gen. Vandegrift. When the 1st Division opened the Allied offensive in the Pacific, landing on the Solomons on August 7, 1942, Rupertus was an assistant division commander and led a successful attack on Tulagi, Gavutu, and the Tanambogo Islands. Two months later, at a ceremony on Guadalcanal, Adm. Nimitz awarded him the Navy Cross for his leadership in the seizure of those islands. Part of his citation read:

For exposing himself frequently and fearlessly to enemy fire and for setting an outstanding example of calmness and courage.

In 1943, when Gen. Vandegrift assumed command of the newly created 1st Marine Amphibious Corps, Gen. Rupertus took command of the 1st Division Marines. He brought a firsthand, thorough knowledge of operations in the Southwest Pacific. In a string of brilliant victories from December 28, 1943, to April 1944, which involved many secondary amphibious operations and bloody battles, the 1st Marine Division, under his leadership, cleared the western part of New Britain and drove the enemy back to Rabaul.

During the Cape Gloucester operations, his careful use of Marine scouts and air maps allowed ground troops to take a nearly undefended route to the Cape Gloucester airfields. After the campaign, Gen. MacArthur went ashore to personally thank Rupertus for the valor of his division and awarded him the Army's distinguished service medal for "exceptionally meritorious and distinguished service during an undertaking fraught with hazard." Part of his citation read:

Gen. Rupertus overcame great difficulties of weather and terrain. After firmly establishing a beachhead between two large enemy forces, he brilliantly maneuvered his troops to destroy each other in turn. While the stubbornly resisting enemy had every advantage of terrain and established offenses, he inflicted on it disproportionate losses of a 10 to 1 ratio. The skillful and courageous leadership of Gen. Rupertus was largely responsible for the success of this bold extension of our operations.

In November 1944, after the Peleliu Campaign, he returned to the US. He was appointed the Commandant of the Marine Corps School in Quantico, Virginia.

He died of a heart attack on March 25, 1945 and was buried at Arlington National Cemetery among family members.

LIEUTENANT COLONEL LEWIS WALT

Lewis William Walt, "Lew Walt," was born on February 16, 1913, in Wabaunsee County, Kansas. Walt graduated from Colorado State University in 1936 with a degree in chemistry. After graduation, he was commissioned as a second lieutenant in the Army Field Artillery Reserve. He resigned that commission to accept an appointment as a Marine second lieutenant on July 6, 1936.

After Lieut. Walt completed The Basic School at Philadelphia in April 1937, he was assigned to the 6th Marine Regiment in San Diego, California, as a machine-gun platoon leader. He embarked for China in August 1937, where he took part in defense of Shanghai's International Settlement until February 1938, when he returned to San Diego. In June 1939, he began his second overseas tour when he was assigned to the Marine Barracks on Guam in the Mariana Islands. Here he was promoted to first lieutenant in October 1939.

After returning to the US in June 1941, before the entry into World War II, Lieut. Walt was assigned as a company commander in the Officer Candidates Class at the Marine Corps School in Quantico, Virginia. Here he was promoted to captain.

In early 1942, Captain Walt volunteered to join the 1st Marine Raider Battalion and was stationed with the battalion on Samoa. On August 7, 1942, as commander of Company A, 1st Raider Battalion, he landed his company on Tulagi for the assault in the British Solomon Islands. He was awarded the Silver Star for his conspicuous gallantry during this landing. After the action, he joined the 5th Marines on Guadalcanal, where he took part in combat as Commanding Officer of the 2/5 Marines. He was promoted to major in September 1942.

In October 1942, Major Walt was wounded in action but continued to fight. Two months later, he was promoted to lieutenant colonel, on the spot, for his distinguished leadership and gallantry in action during the Guadalcanal Campaign.

Following hospitalization and rehabilitation in Australia, LtCol. Walt led the 2/5 Marines in the assault on Cape Gloucester. In the middle of the campaign, he was ordered to take command of the 3/5 Marines during an intense battle for Aogiri Ridge. He earned his first Navy Cross during this action, and Aogiri Ridge was renamed "Walt's Ridge" by Gen. Shepherd. After leaving Cape Gloucester in late February 1944, LtCol. Walt was ordered to the Naval Hospital in Oakland, California, to treat his malaria.

In June 1944, he returned to action in the Pacific Theater. That September, he landed with the Marine force on Peleliu as Regimental Executive Officer of the 5th Marines. On the first day of the battle, he was again ordered to command the 3/5 Marines after the battalion's CO and XO were wounded. After dark on the first day of fighting, three battalion companies had failed to contact the command post, and their whereabouts were unknown. At significant risk to himself, LtCol. Walt went into enemy territory in the middle of the night and located the missing companies. He directed them to their correct position along the divisional line. For these actions, LtCol. Walt was awarded his second Navy Cross.

In November 1944, Walt returned to the US and assumed duty as Chief of the Marine Officer Candidates' School Tactics Section.

Gen. Walt died at 76 years old on March 26, 1989, in Gulfport, Mississippi. He was buried in Quantico National Cemetery.

GARAND M-1 RIFLE

AFTER THE GUADALCANAL CAMPAIGN, the 1st Marine Division received the M-1 rifle. This new rifle was designed by John Garand, a civilian employee from the Springfield Armory in Massachusetts. This weapon was semiautomatic, gas-operated, and weighed 9.5 pounds with an eight-round clip. While less accurate at a longer range than the former standard rifle, the M-1903, which Marine snipers continued to use, the M-1 Garand could lay down a deadly volume of fire at a short range typical to jungle warfare.

The M-1 used a .30-06 round and was the first semiautomatic rifle to be generally issued to any nation's infantry. In November 1941, the Marine Corps classified the M-1 as its standard service rifle. Its bayonet was an M-1905 bayonet. Several Marines resisted the Garand at first because they had become used to the Springfield rifle for almost 30 years. The Springfield was well-respected because of its long-range accuracy and reliability under the harshest of battlefield conditions.

The M-1 Garand gave Marine riflemen a superior firepower advantage against the Japanese opponent, who carried Arisaka Type 99s, which were among the best bolt-action rifles of the war.

Reliable and easy to maintain in the field, an M-1-equipped Marine rifle platoon could sustain the same volume of fire as a full company armed with bolt-action rifles. Operation of the M-1 was simple. Ammo loaded with an eight-round clip inserted into the top of the receiver. When the rifleman fired his last round, the bolt locked to the rear, and the empty clip ejected with a unique *ping*. Reloading, the rifleman simply pushed another loaded clip into the top of the receiver. Once the clip was fully inserted, it unlocked the bolt which stripped off the first round to load in the chamber.

A common problem experienced by new shooters was known as the "M-1 thumb," which happened when the rifleman failed to quickly take his thumb off the clip as he loaded. When the bolt unlocked, it could smash a shooter's thumb against the front of the ejection port. This usually only happened once for most new shooters. While the M-1 had some minor deficiencies, it was without question the finest service rifle of World War II. Marines who carried it in combat swore by its reliability, simplicity, and hard-hitting firepower. It served the Marine Corps well in Korea and through many years of the Cold War until retired from service in the early 1960s.

PIPER L-4 GRASSHOPPER

THE 1ST MARINE Division had an air force of their own at Cape Gloucester. It consisted of a dozen Piper L-4 Grasshoppers provided by the Army. This improvised air force could trace its origins back to the summer of 1943, before the division plunged into the hellish inferno on New Britain.

Captain Petras was Gen. Vandegrift's personal pilot. He devised a plan that would acquire light aircraft for artillery spotting. Gen. Rupertus had seen the Army troops making use of the Piper Grasshoppers on maneuvers. He presented the plan to Gen. MacArthur, who promised to give the 1st

Marine Division twelve Piper Grasshoppers for their next operation.

When the 1st Marine Division arrived off the south-western tip of New Guinea to prepare for further combat, Gen. Rupertus directed Petras to organize an aviation unit from among the Marines. The call went out for volunteers with aviation experience. Out of sixty candidates, twelve were qualified as pilots in the new Air Liaison Unit. When the dozen Piper L-4 Grasshoppers arrived as promised, six proved to be in excellent condition while three needed repairs. The remaining three were only fit to provide parts to keep the others flying.

Nine flyable planes practiced a variety of tasks during the two months of training. Afterward, airmen gained experience in radio communications, artillery spotting, and snagging messages hung in a container trailing a pennant to help the pilot see it from a line strung between two poles.

The division's air force landed at Cape Gloucester from LSTs on D-Day. After reassembling the aircraft, they were put into action. The radios installed in the Piper Grasshoppers were too balky for artillery spotting. The pilots concentrated on courier flights, photographic reconnaissance, and delivering small amounts of cargo.

Piper Grasshoppers could drop a case of dry rations with pinpoint accuracy from an altitude of 200 feet. These light planes could also become attack aircraft when pilots or observers rained hand grenades onto enemy positions.

The Piper L-4 Grasshopper evolved from the civilian plane the Piper J-3 Cub, which was the name most military personnel referred to it as. The only differences were the paint color, and more windows for better visibility. Mechanically, however, they were one and the same. There was room for a pilot in front and a spotter and radio in back, who could perform reconnaissance duties, looking out the extended windows.

The Piper L-4 Grasshopper was not armed, nor armored, which made it vulnerable to antiaircraft guns, but allowed it to fly at low altitudes and low speeds, giving it ideal maneuverability for observation and transportation of supplies and information. It was used in both the Pacific and European Theaters.

FORTRESS OF RABAUL

At Simpson Harbor on the northeastern tip of New Britain, Rabaul served as a naval and air base. It was also a troop staging area for Japanese conquests in New Guinea and the Solomon Islands.

Shortly after the attack on Pearl Harbor, Rabaul was captured by thousands of Japanese naval landing forces. Once the Japanese had seized Rabaul, they got to work converting it into a significant installation. They improved the harbor facilities and built barracks and airfields. They brought in hundreds of thousands of soldiers, airmen, and sailors, who either passed through the base en route to operations elsewhere or stayed to defend it. The Japanese Army dug hundreds of kilometers of tunnels to shelter from Allied air attacks. They also expanded the facilities by constructing Army barracks and support structures. By 1943 there were over 110,000 troops based on Rabaul.

After MacArthur escaped from the Philippines and assumed command of the Southwest Pacific Area, Rabaul became his dominant objective. MacArthur proposed a two-pronged advance on the fortress, bombing it from the air while amphibious forces closed in through eastern New Britain and the Solomon Islands.

When the Allies began to close their pincers on Rabaul, the strategy changed. Through MacArthur's opposition, the American Joint Chiefs decided to bypass the stronghold. As a result, Rabaul remained in Japanese hands for the rest of the war, though the Allies controlled the rest of New Britain.

THE JUNGLE BATTLEFIELD

THROUGHOUT THE CAMPAIGN, the 1st Marine Division fought the terrain, weather, and an unyielding Japanese enemy. Seasonal monsoon rains fell with the velocity of a firehose, soaking everyone, sending streams from their banks, and turning trails into muddy quagmires. The volcanic island terrain varied from coastal plain to mountains that rose as high as 7,000 feet above sea level. The forest-covered island was punctuated by grasslands, large coconut plantations, and garden plots near scattered villages.

Much of the fighting in the early days raged in swamp forests, sometimes described as damp flats. The swamp forests consisted of scattered trees growing as high as a hundred feet from a plane that remained flooded throughout the rainy season—if not the entire year. Tangled roots braced the towering trees but could not anchor them against gale-force winds when vines and undergrowth reduced visibility on the flooded surfaces to only a few yards.

The vegetation in the mangrove forest was no less formidable. Gigantic trees grew from brackish water deposited at high tide. The mangrove trees varied in height from thirty to sixty feet. They had a visible tangle of thick roots as high as ten feet up the trunk holding the tree solidly in place. Underneath the mangrove canopy, a maze of roots wandered through streams and standing water and impeded movement —this limited visibility to less than fifteen yards.

Both the swamp and mangrove forest grew at sea level. Another form of vegetation was the tropical rain forests that flourished at higher altitudes. Different trees formed an impenetrable double canopy overhead. The surface generally remained open except for low growing ferns or an occasional thicket of vines. Marines walking beneath the canopy could see a standing man as far as fifty yards away. A prone rifleman could remain invisible at a distance of only ten yards.

RAIN AND BITING INSECTS

Monsoon winds drove rain that drenched the entire island and everyone on it. At the front, heavy rains flooded foxholes. Conditions weren't much better toward the rear where men slept in jungle hammocks slung between two trees. A Marine would enter his hammock through an opening in a mosquito net and lay down on a rubberized cloth, zipping the net shut. Above him, enclosed in the netting, stretched a rubberized cover designed to shelter him from the rain. Fierce gales like the one that ripped through on the night of D-Day would set the cover flapping like a loose sail and drive the rain inside the hammock.

In the darkness, gusts of winds could uproot trees, weakened by flooding or bombardment, and send them crashing down. A falling tree toppling onto a hammock occupied by one of the Marines could drown him if someone did not slash the covering with a knife.

The rain was like a waterfall pouring down. The first storm lasted five days, and the next storms lasted for weeks. Wet uniforms never dried. Marines continually suffered from fungus infections and jungle rot, which developed into open sores. Mosquito-borne malaria also threatened the Marines' health. They had to contend with aggressive insects: Little red ants, little black ants, and giant red ants on an island where even the caterpillars bite. The Japanese may have endured even more because of medicine shortages and difficulty in distribution, but this was a minor consolation to the Marines beset by disease and discomfort. By the end of January 1944, non-battle injuries or illness had forced over 1,000 Marines to evacuate.

The island's jungles and swamps would have been an ordeal enough without the added rain, wind, and disease. At times, the tormented Marine could see only a few feet in front of him. Movement was nearly impossible, especially with rains flooding the land and turning the volcanic soil into slippery mud. Gen. Shepherd compared the New Britain Campaign to "Grant's fight through the Wilderness in the Civil War."

* * *

Building a relationship with my readers is one of the best things about writing. I occasionally send out emails with details on new releases and special offers. If you'd like to join my free readers group and never miss a new release, go to danielwrinn.com to sign up for the list.

REFERENCES

Information about Bullets and Barbed Wire is vast, and the information I gathered for this book came from several sources. The USMC archives maintained by the Washington National Records Group in Suitland, Maryland, were a source of reference information as well as websites, newspaper articles, and even History Channel documentaries.

First-hand accounts, as recorded by the surviving participants, also contributed to my research. I've cited the main reference books used below:

Once a Marine: The Memoirs of General A. A. Vandegrift, USMC (New York: W. W. Norton, 1964)

Marine: The Life of Chesty Puller (Boston: Little, Brown, 1962)

The Old Breed: A History of the 1st Marine Division in World War II (Washington: Infantry Journal Press, 1949)

The Struggle for Guadalcanal: History of United States Naval Operations in World War II, Vol V (Boston: Little, Brown, 1950)

The Rising Sun: The Decline and Fall of the Japanese Empire 1936-1945 (366 Random House New York 1970)

Galvanic: Beyond the Reef—Tarawa and the Gilberts, Nicholas Roland (Naval History and Heritage Command, 2020.)

The Official Chronology of the U.S. Navy in World War II, Robert J. Cressman (Annapolis, MD/Washington, DC: Naval Institute Press/Naval Historical Center, 1999.)

Across the Reef: The Marine Assault of Tarawa, Joseph A. Alexander (Quantico, VA: Marine Corps History Division, 1993.)

History of United States Naval Operations in World War II, Vol. VII —Aleutians, Gilberts and Marshalls, June 1942–April 1944, Samuel Eliot Morison, (Boston, MA: Little, Brown and Company, 1951.)

Coral and Blood: The U.S. Marine Corps' Pacific Campaign, Hammel, Eric (Pacifica, California: Pacifica Military History, 2010.)

The Campaign on New Britain, Hough, Frank O.; Crown, John A. (USMC Historical Monograph. Washington, DC: Historical Division, Division of Public Information, Headquarters U.S. Marine Corps. 1952)

Cartwheel: The Reduction of Rabaul. United States Army in World War II, Miller, John, Jr. (The War in the Pacific. Office of the Chief of Military History, U.S. Department of the Army.1959)

ALSO BY DANIEL WRINN

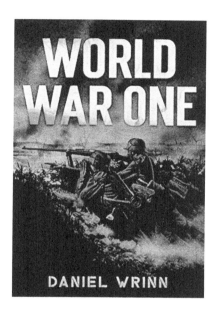

WORLD WAR ONE: WWI HISTORY TOLD FROM THE
TRENCHES, SEAS, SKIES, AND DESERT OF A WAR TORN
WORLD

"Compelling . . . the kind of book that brings history alive." –
Reviewer

**Dive into the incredible history of WWI with
these gripping stories.**

With a unique and fascinating glimpse into the lesser-
known stories of the War to End All Wars, this riveting book
unveils four thrilling stories from the trenches, seas, skies, and
desert of a war-torn world. From one captain's death-defying
mission to smuggle weapons for an Irish rebellion to heroic
pilots and soldiers from all corners of the globe, these stories
shed light on real people and events from one of the greatest
conflicts in human history.

- **WWI: Tales from the Trenches**, a sweeping and eerily realistic narrative which explores the struggles and endless dangers faced by soldiers in the trenches during the heart of WWI
- **Broken Wings**, a powerful and heroic story about one pilot after he was shot down and spent 72 harrowing days on the run deep behind enemy lines
- **Mission to Ireland**, which explores the devious and cunning plan to smuggle a ship loaded with weapons to incite an Irish rebellion against the British
- And **Journey into Eden**, a fascinating glimpse into the lesser-known battles on the harsh and unforgiving Mesopotamian Front

World War I reduced Europe's mightiest empires to rubble, killed twenty million people, and cracked the foundations of our modern world. In its wake, empires toppled, monarchies fell, and whole populations lost their national identities.

Each of these stories brings together unbelievable real-life WWI history, making them perfect for casual readers and history buffs alike. If you want to peer into the past and unearth the incredible stories of the brave soldiers who risked everything, then this book is for you.

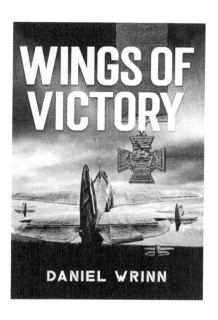

WINGS OF VICTORY: WORLD WAR II ADVENTURES IN A WAR-TORN EUROPE

"Historical fiction with a realistic twist." – Reviewer

Thrilling World War II adventures like you've never seen them before.

As the Nazis invade Europe on a campaign for total domination, a brutal war begins to unfold which will change the course of the world forever—and John Archer finds himself caught in the middle of it. When this amateur pilot joins the Allied war effort and is tasked with a series of death-defying missions which place him deep into German-occupied territory, his hair-raising adventures will help decide the fate of Europe.

In **War Heroes**, John is caught up in the devastating Nazi invasion of France while on vacation. Teaming up with ambulance driver Barney, John will need his amateur pilot skills and more than a stroke of luck to pull off the escape of the century.

In **Bombs Over Britain**, the Nazis have a plan which could change the course of the entire war . . . unless Archer can stop them. Air-dropped into Belgium on a top-secret mission, Archer must retrieve vital intelligence and make it out alive. But that's easier said than done when the Gestapo are closing in.

And in **Desert Scout**, Archer finds himself stranded beneath the scorching Libyan sun and in a race against time to turn the tide of the war in North Africa. But with the Luftwaffe and the desert vying to finish him off, can he make it out alive?

Packed with action and filled to the brim with suspense, these thrilling stories combine classic adventures with a riveting and historical World War II setting, making it ideal for history buffs and casual readers. If you're a fan of riveting war fiction novels, WW2 aircraft, and the war for the skies, Archer's next adventure will keep you on the edge of your seat.

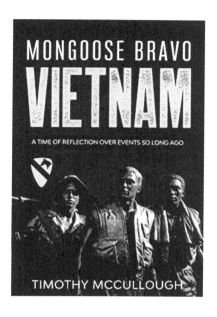

Mongoose Bravo: Vietnam: A Time of Reflection Over
Events So Long Ago

"A frank, real, memoir" – Reviewer

Uncover the gritty, real-life story of a Vietnam combat veteran.

With an engaging and authentic retelling of his experiences as an infantry soldier of the B Co., 1/5th 1st Cavalry Division in the Vietnam War, this gripping account details the life and struggles of war in a strange and foreign country.

What started as a way of bringing closure to a grieving mother morphed into a memoir, covering the author's deployment, duty, and eventual return to the United States after the end of the war. Imbued with the emotion that he felt during this conflicted time, along with letters and journal entries from decades ago, this memoir is a testament to the sacrifice that these brave men and women made fighting on foreign soil.

Recounting the tragedies of war and the chaos of combat as an infantry soldier, in the words of the author: "We lived, and fought as a unit, covering each other's backs. Most came home to tell their own stories, many didn't."

If you like gripping, authentic accounts of life and combat during the Vietnam War, then you won't want to miss Mongoose Bravo: Vietnam: A Time of Reflection Over Events So Long Ago.

ABOUT THE AUTHOR

Daniel Wrinn writes Military History & Action Adventure. A US Navy veteran and avid history buff, Daniel lives in the Utah Wasatch Mountains. He writes every day with a view of the snow capped peaks of Park City to keep him company. You can join his readers group and  get notified of new releases, special offers, and free books here:

www.danielwrinn.com

Made in the USA
Monee, IL
09 August 2021

75297424R00173